Foragers

Illustrated with photographs by the author
and drawings by Nicholas Amorosi

YIWARA:

of the Australian Desert

Richard A. Gould
AMERICAN MUSEUM OF NATURAL HISTORY

Charles Scribner's Sons ⸜ New York

DEDICATED TO THE MEMORY OF

Fay-Cooper Cole

⸗ *Preface* ⸗

"Yiwara" is the word used by the Gibson Desert Aborigines to mean "track." It is in constant use, since it has several levels of meaning. First, at its simplest level, it means the track left by an animal across the sand. From earliest childhood, Aborigines are trained to recognize the tracks of different animals and to follow them to their burrows. It also means the tracks left by people. On the move much of the time in search of food and water, Aborigine families leave tracks as evidence of their passage, and other Aborigines in the region watch for these to see if relatives or newcomers have entered or passed through the area. These are practical applications of the word. It also means the track of a mythical totemic being in the "dreamtime," when such beings are believed by the Aborigines to have transformed themselves into present landmarks of the desert. And, finally, yiwara has come to mean the white man's road or track into the desert, with all the implications this has for change.

Since yiwara epitomizes the hunting and foraging life of the Aborigines, as well as the pervasive element of nomadism in their existence, and also relates to their sacred life, and to the arrival of the white man, the word seemed to me a suitable title for a book which is about all these things. The book is itself a track of the Aborigines' destiny, from the nomadic life of the desert to the more settled and westernized existence on reserves and missions. Experiences and episodes are embedded in this book like tracks in the sand. Just as an Aborigine looks to tracks for clues to the behavior of the animal or persons he is following, so the situations described here may offer clues to understanding these extraordinary people. This is a book about situations in the lives of individuals rather than a formal ethnographic study. I only hope that these people will seem as real and interesting to its readers as they were to me when my wife and I lived with them.

RICHARD A. GOULD

Contents

Illustrations

PHOTOGRAPHS

Note on Aboriginal Terms

In the text, Aboriginal words are italicized on their first appearance; thereafter they are printed in roman type. These words, and other terms such as billabong, mallee, and others which are likely to be unfamiliar to non-Australian readers, are defined briefly in the Glossary. Species names of plants and animals mentioned in the book are given in the Glossary; a few also appear in the text.

A guide to the pronunciation of Aboriginal terms follows.

SOUNDS WITH ENGLISH EQUIVALENTS

a	as in *father*
i	as in *radio*
u	as in *put*
p	as in *pinch*
t	as in *tray*
k	as in *skate*
m	as in *mute*
n	as in *never*
ng	as in *swing*
l	as in *late*
r	a trilled sound like the Scottish *r*
r̪	as in *rip*
w	as in *well*
y	as in *yes*

Sounds with No English Equivalents

a: extended *a* (twice normal length used in English)
i: extended *i* (twice normal length used in English)
u: extended *u* (twice normal length used in English)
ṭ   *t* spoken with tip of tongue turned up
ṇ   *n* spoken with tip of tongue turned up
ḷ   *l* spoken with tip of tongue turned up
ny   a single sound spoken with tongue tip touching teeth
tj   a single sound spoken with tongue tip touching teeth
ly   a single sound spoken with tongue tip touching teeth

ↆ   ↆ   ↆ   YIWARA: *Foragers of the Australian Desert*

A Day with the Desert People

December 28, 1966

The summer heat has reached its full strength, and the sandhills near Partjar seem to be enveloped in a shimmering pink haze. The thermometer I am carrying registers 118 degrees Fahrenheit in the shade. Nothing moves except the flies, yet the sandhills seem to bob and dance as oven-hot air slides over them. I can feel the heat penetrating the soles of my tennis shoes, and drawing a deep breath causes my tongue to dry out like a potato chip. Clearly it was a mistake to go exploring around at midday, and I think it best now to follow the advice of Noel Coward ("Mad dogs and Englishmen go out in the noonday sun") and return to camp. The Aborigines are still snoozing under whatever shade they can find. A couple of little girls,

Nyaputja and Manyi, are splashing in the shallow water of the drowned creekbed. They look like slippery brown eels playing in the mud, but there is no doubt that they have found the coolest place around. This is a good time to sit down, catch up on my note-taking, and await further developments.

Partjaṛ is a veritable oasis in the remote sandhill country. It consists of a series of billabongs or standing pools of water in an otherwise dry creekbed that winds through and out of the Clutterbuck Hills in the heart of the Gibson Desert about 150 miles northwest of the Warburton Ranges. The billabongs here hold water for most of the year. Even when the water on the surface evaporates, water can still be reached by digging into the soft mud at the bottom of the creekbed. In the summer and during times of drought individual families of Aborigines fall back on Partjaṛ as a dependable watering place and a base from which to hunt and forage. The Clutterbuck Hills lie almost on a line between the Rawlinson Range and the Alfred and Marie Range, so the explorer Ernest Giles must have passed close to this place on his final push to the west from Circus Water in 1874. How much misery he would have been spared had he known about this series of waterholes.

Living in the desert with a nomadic family group of thirteen Nyatunyatjara people has given me a fine opportunity to observe many of the things I came here to study: tool-making, hunting and butchering of game, social relationships, and other activities pertinent to my research. My personal reasons for being here, however, go beyond these research objectives. I know now that what I really wanted was to experience the tempo and detail of the hunting and foraging way of life. Societies in which people live entirely by hunting and foraging are rare today, and the few that remain—for example, the Bushmen of the Kalahari Desert in South Africa, the Forest Pygmies of the Congo, and the desert Aborigines of Australia—are being subjected to contact with Europeans that will soon change them. Human history was tied up with this kind of economy from the time of *Australopithecus* and the fossil hominids of Olduvai Gorge in East Africa over a million and a half years ago until the beginnings of agriculture within the last nine or ten thousand years. With the spread of agriculture, only a few societies continued to live by hunting and foraging, and these mainly in climates inhospitable to farming. Some, such as the Arctic Eskimo, the Paiute Indians of western North America, and a few Yahgan and Alacaluf Indians on the coast of Tierra del Fuego, managed to cling to their traditional economy until the end of the nineteenth century and into the early twentieth. But with current trends in world history, hunting and gathering as a full-time means of livelihood seems doomed to disappear from the world during the later decades of the twentieth century.

Thus the few anthropologists who are currently studying living hunter-gatherers will be among the last people on earth actually to observe this way of life first hand. These few years, seen in terms of the whole range of human history, comprise an extraordinary moment in time. It is still possible for people with a nuclear technology to catch a final glimpse of this traditional mode of life. There is so much to learn and feel before the time is irrevocably past. This is the reason that I came to the Gibson Desert, and that some of my colleagues are in the tropical forests of the Congo and the desert scrublands of the Kalahari. For us, living and sharing experiences with these nomadic peoples is exhilarating but carries with it an inescapable feeling of loss, as if we were watching the last redwood or the last bison disappear. This is how it feels to be an anthropologist living with the Aborigines in the Gibson Desert of Australia on December 28, 1966.

Foraging and Hunting

Action at the camp begins with the first faint glow of sunrise. It will still be dark for another half hour, but while the air is cool and there is no wind the birds do most of their singing, and there is conversation and joking in camp. Children are given wooden bowls and sent to fetch water. They have done this so often in the last month that there is now a narrow little trail running from the camp to the waterhole. When they return everyone has a drink and takes a few bites from the seedcakes that the women prepared yesterday. The flies are not very active yet, so this is the most comfortable part of the day and a good time to make plans.

The senior member of the group is Mitapuyi, a man about forty-five years old. There are three adult women: Nyurapaya, Mitapuyi's wife; Tjanangu, a widow, Mitapuyi's younger sister; and Katapi, wife of Walanya, the other adult male in the group and Mitapuyi's brother-in-law;[1] as well as a girl about fifteen years old, Tjukapaṭi, Mitapuyi's eldest and as yet unmarried daughter. The children include Yuma (aged about ten), only son of Mitapuyi and Nyaputja, their younger daughter (about six); Manyi, Tjanangu's only daughter (about twelve); and Katapi's four children by her first husband, now deceased: Tanara (daughter, about thirteen), Tana (son, about eleven), Nuṇi (son, about eight), and Ngampakatju (son, about four). These individuals, all related, comprise a group somewhat larger and including more different kinds of relatives than the average American family, fairly typical of the small family aggregates of Aborigines which set up camps at more or less permanent waterholes and forage together during dry seasons.

The talk about the activities for the day goes on for a long time. From time to time a person takes a drink of water or a bit of food or retires to micturate. The women and girls generally go off a few yards into the bush for this function, but the men often urinate right where they sit, in camp. The men have decided to hunt emus, so the discussion centers around what the women will do. Nyurapaya has decided that her bark sandals are worn out and need to be replaced. During the day the sand becomes too hot to walk around on comfortably barefoot, so these sandals (called *palykanpa*) get lots of use. Sandals are made from the green bark of *taliwanti*, a plant which grows in the sandhills. Nyurapaya knows where to find some of these plants, but the place lies in a different direction from the area where the women have lately been looking for edible plants. Should they take a chance that they will come across some edible seeds or fruit on the way to the taliwanti-place? Or should they stick with a sure thing and manage with their worn-out sandals for another day?

Nyurapaya wants new sandals, but she is shy and hates to

assert herself in discussions, and Tjanangu feels the same way. Katapi, on the other hand, is both intelligent and forceful in expressing her views. She thinks it would be better to finish collecting seeds at their established place and wait a few days for the sandals. She is cautious and would rather make full use of the resources at hand than go off to a new and untried area. Nyurapaya and Tjanangu have made their wishes known and are reluctant to press the matter further. In situations like this, Katapi's views are usually accepted, and this time is no exception. Nyurapaya sighs and wiggles a finger through one of the holes in the more worn of her two sandals. She sees the sense in what Katapi says and will go along, but she would still like new sandals.

These sandals are important to me, however, since they have been reported only twice before from any Aboriginal group in Australia.[2] I am determined not to let this opportunity slip by, since I very much want to see how the sandals are made. I tell the women that I will give them some plugs of chewing tobacco in exchange for their old sandals and any extra new ones they might make. Ordinarily the desert Aborigines collect supplies of wild tobacco (*mingkulpa* or *tjuntiwari*—both species of true *Nicotiana*). which they sun-dry and chew, often mixed with ashes, but lately neither kind has been available near Partjar. Thus my offer is attractive, and discussion begins anew. As usual, it is Katapi who solves the problem and makes the decision. She remembers a sandy flat beyond the taliwanti-place where she thinks they may find some ripe *ngaru* (fruit of the shrub *Solanum eremophilum*). Her opinion is that the other women should proceed to the taliwanti place while she goes on ahead to look for ngaru. If she is successful, she will send up a smoke signal, and the others can follow. Otherwise, she will rejoin them. Her view is immediately accepted by the others, and they decide to start at once, since they will have a long walk across many sandhills.

Mitapuyi and Walanya decide to proceed in the opposite direction, into the Clutterbuck Hills, to a spot along the creekbed where they have set up a brush blind. They will wait there for emus. Since they plan to hunt from concealment (the preferred method for hunting kangaroos and emus in the desert country north of the Warburton Ranges), they decide to let the women take the dogs. The group has six dingoes, all scrawny-looking but treated with affection by their owners. The dogs are not trained in any way and would only interfere with the hunters and frighten away the game with their barking. The two men pick up their spears and spearthrowers and head south toward the gap in the hills where the hunting blind lies. Mitapuyi has killed five emus in this area in the last three months—an exceptionally good record—and today he hopes to spear another of these big birds.

Meanwhile the women gather up digging-sticks and four large wooden bowls. These fine deep bowls, called *ngunma*, are intended to carry enough drinking water for the trip out. One bowl even has a spinifex-resin spout fashioned at one end to make it easier to drink from. Each bowl is filled with water, and a twisted piece of grass is placed in the water to reduce the sloshing. Each woman has a little doughnut-shaped loop of human hair-string which she places on her head to cushion and steady the load, and with this in place, the filled bowls are hoisted up and put in position. After a bit of hip-and-shoulder wriggling the loads are set, and the women start off, with the children and dogs. They head northward, directly toward the sandhills. Just as they are leaving camp, Katapi rushes back to get a lighted firestick, a piece of smoldering mulga wood which she carries with her. Campfires are left burning, and odd pieces of seedcake and other food are placed in a wooden bowl up in a tree. In addition to the firestick and the load on her head, Katapi carries her little son Ngamapakatju on one hip, steadying him with her free arm. By six o'clock the camp is empty.

One nice thing about getting away from camp is there are fewer flies about. Offal tends to accumulate around a campsite, providing the main fare for the dogs. Animal bones, after they have been shattered for marrow, are tossed out at random and accumulate literally a "bone's throw" from the living areas. Scraps of food, feces, and other litter also accumulate nearby, and before long the area swarms with flies. Though remarkably healthy in most other respects, the nomadic Aborigines suffer from boils and eye ailments, all occasioned by the flies and dust. Intestinal problems can also arise this way. For the anthropologist living in or alongside an Aboriginal camp these factors constitute an ever-present occupational hazard. Nyurapaya and her little daughter Nyaputja are both suffering from painful eye infections, and Katapi has a large boil on one foot. The quest for food must go on, however, so such painful ailments are generally borne with an outward display of good cheer. Only Nyaputja complains, but the others admit she is still a child and has not yet learned discipline. My stores of simple remedies like aspirin and ointments are probably the most welcome aspect of my presence here.

Mitapuyi and Walanya do not have far to go today. The circular brush blind (*manngu*) is only a little over a mile from camp, in a shallow rocky glen next to the creekbed. The blind is about six feet in diameter with sides about thirty inches high, and it lies on the bank three feet above the floor of the creekbed. Choosing a dry spot in the gravelly creekbed the hunters dig a small hole, continuing their digging until the hole fills with water seeping in from just below the surface. The small soakhole lies only about twenty feet from the blind.

Here the two men lie quietly, hoping that the emus will not find some other route by which to approach the big billabongs farther downstream. They have seen fresh tracks in the creekbed, indicating that the big birds have passed this way recently. A small mulga tree shades the blind, which is fortunate, since the morning heat builds up rapidly. Both men chew plugs of tobacco that they have stored behind their ears. The tobacco acts as a mild narcotic, and it also helps moisten their mouths against the hot dry air.

The hours creep by as the men wait motionless. It takes intense discipline to keep from fidgeting in a situation like this, particularly with the flies all around. Around eleven o'clock their vigil is rewarded by a low booming note from just around an upstream bend. This is a sure sign that an emu is approaching, and both men quietly engage their spears to the spearthrowers. As Mitapuyi lies poised with his spearthrower, the emu appears about a hundred feet away, walking slowly and looking from side to side. It approaches the water slowly, stopping and cautiously looking before moving closer. By now the excitement in the blind is almost too much to bear, and, finally, with the bird about thirty feet away, Mitapuyi rises smoothly to his feet and lifts his spearthrower. Although Walanya is ready beside him, both men know there will be a chance for only one shot. As the spear is thrown, there is a loud snap. The force of Mitapuyi's throw has caused the spearshaft to break, and the broken spear misses. Now the alerted emu wastes no time in dashing away.

The fault lay with the new spear Mitapuyi was using. The shaft was made from a mulga branch collected only a short time ago. Mulga generally is poor wood for making spears, especially when collected during a dry season. It tends to be brittle and can snap unexpectedly, as this shaft just did. Mitapuyi and Walanya decide to make some better spears at the earliest opportunity. They try to laugh the whole thing off, but there is no doubt that they are disappointed.

Realizing that no more emus are likely to come now, the two men start the walk back to camp. Along the way, Walanya picks up the fresh tracks of *kurkaṭi*, a kind of goanna not often seen at this place. The two men speedily follow out the trail

Emu hunting at Partjaṛ in the Clutterbuck Hills.

as it winds and twists between clumps of spinifex, reaching the hole after about ten minutes of tracking. By peering into the hole they can see what direction the lizard has taken inside the burrow. Walanya stamps on the ground about three feet from the burrow, to crush the lizard's tunnel and trap him close to the entrance. Meanwhile, Mitapuyi grabs a stick from the ground nearby and uses it to dig into the burrow. Kurkaṭi is always easy to catch. This one was only about a foot underground, and Mitapuyi grabs it by the tail and pulls it out within a minute of starting to dig. The lizard is quickly killed with a blow on its head with the stick, and Mitapuyi tucks it into his hair-string belt to carry it back to camp. This is a small lizard, weighing only three pounds, but in other parts of the desert these lizards can grow much larger. This small catch has redeemed the hunting trip, and Mitapuyi is extremely pleased. The men arrive back in camp a little before noon.

The women have much farther to go. They walk erect, with an easy grace that is difficult to describe because it is so unlike the way Americans and Europeans move. Their movements are flowing, and they seem hardly to exert themselves at all. Yet for all my struggling I can barely keep up with them. I notice they do not dig the soles of their feet into the ground as they walk, the way I do, but place their feet down fairly flat. Only Katapi digs in her heel, and I can see she is favoring her sore foot. There is a lot of talk and laughter along the way, some of it directed at me. No doubt they find my slow and jerky movements in the sand quite comical. The children are having a grand time, racing ahead or off to the side, chasing tiny lizards that dart out from under the spinifex. Little Ngampakatju is running alongside now, racing after lizards with the others. Despite his small size, he has no trouble keeping up. The dogs, too, go racing after these tiny lizards, devouring them whole whenever they catch them. The children catch a few, which they give to the dogs.

We have come a long way. So far the ground has been sandy but perfectly level. The Clutterbuck Hills are now faintly visible as a thin horizontal stripe of pale purple on the southern horizon. Just as we approach the first sandhill there is a shout from off

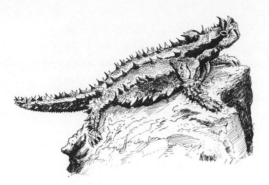

The "mountain devil" lizard
(*ngiyaṛi*), formidable-looking
but harmless.

to one side, and Nuṇi runs up, clutching a small lizard he has
caught. This is *ngiyaṛi,* a fantastically fierce-looking little animal
covered with sharp spines and brightly colored in a mottled pattern of reddish-brown, yellow, and black. Because of its appearance, white Australians call it the "mountain devil," though in
fact it is altogether harmless. Nuṇi is totally delighted with his
new plaything and places it on his head. The animal quickly
burrows into his long hair and settles down while Nuṇi runs off
after more lizards.

I am not a good judge of distances, but it feels as if we
have walked about five or six miles. A shrill, falsetto shout, *"Puyi!"*
from Nyurapaya indicates that she has found taliwanti plants
on top of a large sandhill. There is nothing spectacular about
these plants. They are fairly straight-stemmed, with a pale whit-
ish-green color to the bark and leaves, and stand only about two
or three feet high. The women pull off the leaves and remove
long strips of bark. While this collecting goes on, Katapi continues to the north, disappearing rapidly over the next sandhill,
on her way to look for ngaṛu. She is still carrying her lighted
firestick.

The women take only as much bark as they plan to use,
leaving many taliwanti plants in the area untouched. After about
twenty minutes of collecting they stop and drink from one of the
wooden bowls. When the bowl is about two-thirds empty, they
wad the bark together into bundles and place it in the bowl,
then put the bowl in the shade of a small bush. This keeps the
bark moist and supple. Then we all sit down together under a

ridiculously small tree, taking advantage of what little shade there is to be had. Nuṇi gives his new pet to Ngampakatju, and the two children play with it for a while, letting it run back and forth between their legs. They seem like small children at play anywhere in the world. Suddenly Nuṇi seizes the live lizard and tears off a leg. Ngampakatju grabs it and does the same, and for a few moments the two children giggle with delight as they tear the animal to pieces. Their mothers and the other children find this hilarious. I smile weakly but admit to myself that I will probably never become accustomed to such sudden manifestations of cruelty among these otherwise gentle people. There is nothing unusual about small children anywhere treating animals in this way, but it is disconcerting to see adults take such delight in it, too.

"*Puyu nyaratja* [Smoke over there, in the distance]!" We have all been looking to the north, but it is Nuṇi who sees the smoke first. It appears as a translucent wisp of blue-gray just above the tops of the sandhills. Soon it rises higher, but by this time we are all on our way again, following Katapi's tracks in the sand.

A situation like this explains some popular misunderstandings about Aboriginal smoke signals. I have heard individuals describe complex and detailed messages that they have seen transmitted in this way, and they sometimes expressed surprise or awe at the amount of information a simple puff of smoke could convey. Of course, what usually happens is just what happened today—the sender and receiver agree beforehand on what the signal will mean. If an outsider were to appear now and ask one of the women what the smoke meant, he would probably be told something like: "That's Katapi. She says she has found some ripe ngaṛu, and we should come and gather it." This would naturally impress an observer who had not been present when the meaning of the signal was agreed on.

The sandhills here are laced with the tracks of small animals, and the children draw me off incessantly to point out the tracks and tell me what animal made them. Sometimes one can have too much of a good thing, and this is my plight right now. I cannot stop to take notes, and I have left my handbook of snakes and lizards in camp, so I cannot make identifications, yet

I am interested in what the children have to say. They are proud
of their knowledge. Before long Nyurapaya and Tjanangu, not
to be outdone, also start showing me tracks and telling me names.
By the time we meet Katapi again I feel as if I have been figura-
tively drowned in a deluge of names for every animal that crawls
or hops across the sandhills in the Gibson Desert.

Katapi has done very well indeed. Not only has she located
a fine patch of ripe ngaṛu, but she has also found some bushes
containing dried *kampuṛarpa* fruit. When they are ripe, the fruits
of both kampuṛarpa and ngaṛu look like diminutive green toma-
toes. Ngaṛu generally has a more tart flavor, but both are staples
for the desert people. They ripen at opposite times of year: ngaṛu
around December-January and kampuṛarpa around July-August.
However, under dry conditions, kampuṛarpa fruits do not rot but
dry out in the hot sun until they acquire the appearance of large
raisins hanging on the bush. This is how they look now, and in
this desiccated state they are edible and highly prized.

Before the heavy work of collecting gets under way, everyone takes a long drink, emptying all the wooden bowls as well
as the two-gallon waterbag I have brought with me. Then the
three women and Tjukapaṭi fan out into the bushes to collect
the fruit. Ngaṛu is simply picked ripe from the bush, but for the
dry kampuṛarpa it is easier to shake the bush until the fruit drops
onto the ground beneath, then gently pull the fruit together into
a pile and scoop it into a bowl. As the wooden bowls are filled,
the sides are built up with bunches of grass and sticks, almost
doubling the capacity of each vessel. During this time the children continue their play, chasing lizards and now and then picking some fruit, either in play or helping their mothers. Little
Ngampakatju is particularly keen on this, returning time after
time with armloads of ngaṛu, even after his mother's bowl is
completely full. Katapi acts delighted, giving him encouragement
to collect more, even though she will have to leave most of it
behind.

Nyurapaya brings out a small stick which she has been carrying in her hair. Katapi does the same. The sticks are about six
inches long, flat, sharp, and shiny from use. They are called *pangara,* and they are used with a single deft wrist motion to split
the husk of each ngaṛu fruit and remove the seeds. Only the thin

outer husk of ngaṟu is eaten. The children eat some while waiting for the women to finish collecting. The three big bowls are completely filled in less than an hour, with a total of between thirty-five and forty pounds of fruit.

The journey back to camp begins immediately. Now the children are less playful, for the sun is hotter and they are tired. The women are tired, too, and talk much less on the return trip. But they continue to move rapidly and smoothly across the sand and do not once stop to rest. Ngampakatju wants his mother to carry him, but this she cannot do because of the large and shaky load on her head. He must learn to walk with the rest of the children. Back by the tree where we sat earlier, Tjukapaṭi retrieves the bowl full of taliwanti bark and then races to catch up with the rest of the group. At first I do not understand the need for haste, but Katapi enlightens me by explaining: *"Piriya kuḷi pitja-pungkula—witjama* [The hot wind is coming with force— keep moving quickly]." Speaking in this way implies real urgency, and even now I can see a few spinifex tassels start to wave as the first breeze hits them. I have already experienced the fierce drying heat of the midday wind off the sandhills and know what she means. No one says very much now, for all are intent on quickly getting back to camp where there is a bit of shade and shelter from the wind. We arrive soon after noon, with the wind at our backs but in time to avoid its worst effects, and everyone is glad to take a long drink of water and lie in the shade for a while. The men, who have been back nearly an hour, are roasting the goanna in the coals of a small fire. Mitapuyi talks excitedly about the emu that got away.

We are all tired and even irritable after the long hot trek. Ngampakatju feeds for a while from Katapi's breast. Aborigine children are indulged to an extreme degree, and sometimes continue to suckle until they are four or five years old. Physical punishment for a child is almost unheard of. But today Ngampakatju goes too far. After nursing he races over to where the other children are playing and goes into a tantrum. He is ignored until he starts throwing sand in everyone's eyes. At this point Katapi takes the almost unprecedented action of cuffing Ngampakatju across the face. She then sits him down beside her, where she can keep an eye on him. Everyone is glad that she has done this, for Aborigine adults generally hate to discipline children, and will avoid this unpleasant task whenever possible.

As on most days, the hunt has been poor, but the collecting has been successful. Over fifty percent of the diet of these people is regularly made up of vegetable foods drawn mainly from a list of at least eight staples, like ngaṟu and kampuṟarpa, which ripen and become available at different times of year and in different places. In addition, there are other plant foods, such as the *yarnguli* berry (*Santalum lanceolatum*) and *wama,* sugar from the sweet and succulent yellow flower of the shrub *Grevillea eriostachya,* which supplement and add variety to the basic fare. In the sand-hill country meat is generally hard to get. The recent successes in emu hunting are not likely to be repeated for several years, and even in unusually good years large game such as kangaroo and emu constitutes only a small part of the overall diet. Small game is more important as a source of protein, and heading the list are lizards—goannas and the common blue-tongue (*ḻungaṭa*)—as well as some edible grubs and, since Europeans reached Australia, rabbits and feral cats. Lizards are so important to these desert Aborigines that one Australian popular writer has referred to the people as "lizard eaters." [3]

Mitapuyi and Walanya allow the goanna to roast until the coals have cooled. This basic procedure is followed in cooking all meat, regardless of size, though for larger game such as kangaroo, euro (an animal similar to the kangaroo), and emu a shallow trench is dug in the ground, the animal is placed inside on its back, and the hot coals are heaped over it. The coals generally take forty to fifty minutes to cool. This means that small game like goanna tends to be well-done, but larger animals remain exceedingly rare—almost raw by European standards. After being roasted, the animal, regardless of size, is divided and shared. There are complicated rules governing the sharing of meat and other food among various classes of relatives. [4] The basic rule is that each animal is divided into a fixed number of named portions which are offered to the various classes of the hunter's kin present at the division. There is no way of storing meat, so it must be shared as widely as possible and eaten soon before it rots. Certain kinds of kin, such as fathers-in-law and brothers-in-law,

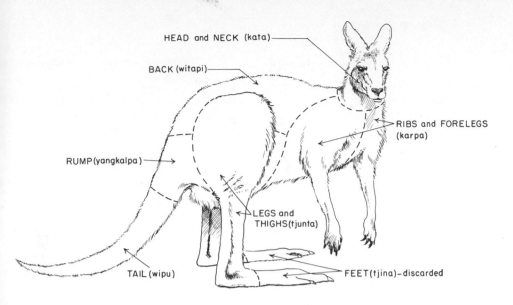

HEAD and NECK (kata)

BACK (witapi)

RIBS and FORELEGS (karpa)

RUMP (yangkalpa)

LEGS and THIGHS (tjunta)

TAIL (wipu)

FEET (tjina)–discarded

How to divide a kangaroo into shares. The dotted lines indicate the pieces into which the animal is divided immediately after it is killed.

have first choice from among the portions, followed then by other classes of kin, like elder and younger brothers, and, last of all, by the hunter himself. These shares in turn are divided by each sharer among his own parents, wives, and children.

At first glance this system of sharing seems unfair to the hunter, who after all got the meat in the first place. Looked at through the eyes of the Aborigines, however, this arrangement actually doubles the rewards to the hunter by giving him both social prestige as a good kinsman and meat, when, according to the same set of rules, he takes *his* share from someone else's catch. When the goanna is cooked, Mitapuyi pulls it from the fire and breaks it into two halves; *kultu* (foresection, including head, forelegs, and about half of the body) and *karilypa* (hindquarters, including the rest of the body, hindlegs, and tail). These he lays on the ground, and Walanya, by virtue of his in-law relationship to Mitapuyi, selects the hindquarters portion. It is interesting to watch these two men in situations where they are sharing food or goods. Walanya has selected the hindquarters, the portion which general opinion regards as the better of the two. He has the right to do this, and his temperament is such that he nearly always asserts his rights when the opportunity arises. He tends almost to be "touchy" about his rights and claims, and, speaking subjectively, this trait perhaps makes him a less appealing personality than Mitapuyi, who is always looking for ways to enhance his reputation as a generous kinsman and a good provider. However, Walanya never pushes his claims so far as to make him liable to accusations of being a *wati manyu-manyu* (a greedy man)—a really serious insult.

The two men then do something I have never seen before. Mitapuyi gets a large, more or less flat cobble from the creek-bed, along with a small one just the right size to hold in one hand. They take their respective shares of the goanna and each in turn lays his share on the large cobble. Finally, using the hand-held stone as a pounder, they mash their shares into pulpy masses, with bone, meat, and skin all shredded together. Only the innards (except for the intestines, which are thrown away) are eaten separately, by Mitapuyi. This is always the hunter's due, and sometimes it is all he gets for his share. This kind of goanna, unlike *ngintaka*, another species inhabiting the region, has a cartilaginous skeleton which can be mashed in this way and eaten along with the meat. Each man hands out a portion of shredded meat and bone to every member of his family. On this occasion, the individual portions are very small, barely a mouthful in fact, but nothing is wasted.

All fleshy foods are called *kuka* by these people, while vegetable and nonfleshy foods are classed as *mirka*. Kuka is always preferred over mirka, but on most days, as with today, mirka is actually more important in the total diet. Since it is the women who collect and prepare most of the mirka, they are thus the mainstay of the economy. For all their talk about this or that kangaroo they once killed, or the pros and cons of a particular spot for hunting, the men contribute relatively little to the subsistence of the group.

One consequence of the preponderance of vegetable over meat foods is a tendency toward an unbalanced diet. There is usually enough to eat, but generally the emphasis is on particular staples, one or two at a time. Thus while the people are strong and basically quite healthy, they sometimes do show signs of deficiencies. This is particularly the case with the children. All the children in this group have strikingly swollen bellies. I cannot offer an expert diagnosis of their condition, but in other parts of the world this symptom can indicate protein deficiencies in the diet. After observing the relatively low protein intake of this group, I am inclined to think this may be the case here, though, alternatively, the condition may be merely swelling caused by the large amount of roughage eaten by children. Whatever the causes, the condition is so common that all desert Aborigines regard it as a normal part of childhood. The condition is called *nungkumunu* (unfilled), and it often leaves stretch-scars which remain throughout adult life. People sometimes proudly point out their scars to me as evidence of the rigors of their childhood.

By now the sun has passed its zenith, and it is the hottest part of the day. The wind is blowing hard, sending up localized whirlwinds (called willy-willys by many Australians and *kupi-kupi* by the desert people), like the "dust-devils" of American deserts. It is a time to conserve one's strength, to take a nap or just lie in the shade. At times like this the small shade-shelters (*wiltja*) here provide more protection from the sun than do the desert trees. There are three of these shelters; Walanya and his family use one, Mitapuyi and his family another, and Tjanangu shares the third with Manyi. These shelters, five or six feet in diameter and constructed in a roughly semicircular plan, take very little time to build. One man can make one in a couple of hours. Branches of mulga are set into dug holes, with the brushy ends upward. The tops of the branches arch over to meet, making what white Australians sometimes call a "humpy." The framework of boughs is given an outer covering of grass, and, as a final step, the interior floor is scooped out to a depth of three or four inches. Simple as the shelters are, the winter camp is an even less complicated affair. During cold weather, all that is needed is a brush windbreak placed around hearths where the people sleep.

About 4:30 the wind suddenly falls off, and the day begins to get cooler. On some days, if the collecting has not been successful; the women go out again at this time to look for food.

But today they decide to stay in camp and prepare the fruits they have collected. Each woman has a stone hand-grinder and a flat rock grinding slab for preparing seeds and berries, and the loads of ngaṟu and kampuṟarpa are placed on these in piles. Katapi goes to work on the kampuṟarpa, while Nyurapaya, Tjanangu, and Tjukapaṭi process ngaṟu.

The desiccated kampuṟarpa fruits are placed on the grinding slab and a small amount of water is poured over them. Then Katapi takes the hand grinder and, with a powerful thrusting motion, proceeds to mash the fruit into a paste. The paste is dark reddish-brown in color and is filled with seeds and grit. While it is still moist, she packs the paste together into a ball which grows larger and larger as she grinds and adds more fruits. The completed balls of paste are about ten inches in diameter, and the outer surface congeals and hardens quickly in the dry heat. Prepared in this way, the paste will keep almost indefinitely. It is put into wooden bowls to be kept until wanted.

Some of the ngaṟu fruit is eaten fresh, but most of it is cleaned and the husks placed in the coals of a small fire. As an alternative to this kind of parching, Tjukapaṭi shows me how ngaṟu can be sun-dried, by placing the husks on a stick which makes it look like pieces of shish kebab on a skewer. Prepared either way, the ngaṟu dry to about the consistency of corn flakes. Parched or sun-dried ngaṟu is eaten after it has been dipped in water and allowed to soften and swell. As a true dehydrated food, it is lightweight and storable and for these reasons is sometimes placed in tree-caches out in the bush for hunters who may have to walk long distances away from camp in search of game. In camp, however, it is usually mixed with water, ground into a paste, and packed into balls in the same manner as kampuṟarpa fruit; it is considered tastier this way. While it is common for Aborigine women to prepare wild vegetable foods by grinding, baking, parching, and in other ways, they cannot be said to have recipes of any kind.

The grinding is hard work and occupies the women almost until dark. There is no fixed mealtime. When food is ready, it is generally shared and eaten, and now the children come and devour handfuls of kampuṟarpa and ngaṟu paste. Meanwhile, the men have retired in the bush to a spot about a quarter-mile from camp. Here there is a small mulga tree which serves as a cache for sacred objects. Women and children are not permitted near this cache, and to warn them off there are sticks placed horizontally in the branches of the trees and several rows of upright rock slabs nearby. Such warning signs are called *nguḻu* (fear, danger); it is thought that sight of or contact with sacred objects can bring instant physical illness or insanity to a woman or an uninitiated male.

Mitapuyi's Magic

Mitapuyi, in addition to his talents as hunter and kinsman, has a reputation as a powerful sorcerer (*mapaṇtjara*). Among the desert Aborigines, a sorcerer may direct his magic toward either beneficial or harmful purposes, as the situation demands. Each sorcerer has a "kit" or bundle of small objects (*mapaṇpa*) which he regards as having potent magical powers. These objects may include natural items like bits of pearl shell, quartz crystals, or tektites (round or dumbbell-shaped glassy objects thought by scientists to be of extraterrestrial origin), or man-made items like old eyeglass lenses acquired somehow from white men. These objects are widely used in curing diseases and in driving away night spirits (*mamu*), both beneficial forms of magic regularly conducted by sorcerers like Mitapuyi. However, on this occasion, it is clear that Mitapuyi intends his magic to be harmful, and I fear that too many direct questions about his intentions will cause him to exclude me from his activities.

He approaches the mulga tree and takes down a flat, double-pointed board about thirty inches long and three inches wide, carved from a slab of mulga wood, which had been stored in a kind of shelf of boughs and twigs. On both sides of this board there is fine carving: concentric circles with connecting lines on one side and a series of intricate interlocking and rectangular hatched designs on the other side. The craftsmanship is extremely good, and the carvings are about three-quarters completed. Mitapuyi must have been working on this object for weeks, yet this is the first time I have seen it. I realize now that on at least some occasions when he and Walanya said they had gone hunting they had been carving this object instead. The others know nothing about it.

The carved board is called *yirilmaṛi*. It looks like any of a number of different kinds of sacred boards which I have seen in the course of preparations for various ceremonies. It, too, I am told, is a sacred board in the same sense as those I have seen already, but it has an important extra use, and that is what concerns Mitapuyi and Walanya now. They are not anticipating any ceremonies. Instead, they plan to use this carved board as a pointing instrument, for magically projecting sickness and death over a long distance to a victim they have selected. Some anthropologists and popular writers have called this kind of activity "pointing the bone," and, indeed, the desert Aborigines often do use for such purposes carved, pointed bones, as well as large pieces of pointed pearlshell or pointed instruments of steatite or some other stone which can be carved in this way.

Most of these instruments are considered so potent that the owner of one purposely avoids pointing it at anyone but his intended victim. Accidental pointing can be dangerous, even to one's relatives and friends. Since sorcery of this kind invites retaliation, the sorcerer generally keeps his preparation secret. Obviously Mitapuyi and Walanya have discussed whether or not to let me see even this much, and I realize that they must trust in my promise not to tell any other Aborigines I meet about their present activities. Although they will not answer questions about the identity of the intended victim or the reason this dire magic is being directed at him, they do not mind talking about sorcery in general or about the way this board works. The sorcerer who operates the magical weapon sings a short song as he points it in the direction of the victim's camp. The malignant power from the weapon flies through the air and enters the victim through one of his body openings. Ideally, pointing is done at close range, while the victim is alone and can be seen, for example at night while he is asleep or when he goes into the bush to defecate.

The two sides of Mitapuyi's lethal *yirilmaṛi* board (approximately one-fourth actual size).

But it is said to work over long distances, too. The victim will soon sicken and may even die.

Mitapuyi is still carving the board, using a stone-tipped engraving tool called *pitjuru-pitjuru*. The wooden handle of this tool is about fifteen inches long, with a spinifex-resin haft at one end for the stone tip and another blob of resin at the other end as a thumb rest. The pitjuru-pitjuru is used only for incising magical and sacred designs; otherwise it too is kept concealed. While Mitapuyi does the carving, using sharp jabbing motions or heavy pressure toward himself to incise the decorative patterns on the surface of the yirilmaṛi, Walanya steadies it for him. The stone tip of the engraving tool is quickly dulled by this hard use, and every two or three minutes Mitapuyi must resharpen it with his teeth. The technique of biting to sharpen a hafted stone flake is widespread among the Aborigines of the Gibson Desert[5] but is not reported from anywhere else in the world today. It will be several days at least before the board is finished, and, given the secrecy surrounding such operations, I doubt that I shall be allowed to watch the actual pointing and "singing" when they take place.

Certain clues, however, lead me to suspect who the victim may be and why he merits such punishment. Several months ago, when the families were living at the Warburton Ranges Mission, a Ngatatjara man who has lived around white settlements for a number of years took Katapi's daughter, Tanara, into the bush for a few days. Sex experience comes early to Aborigine youngsters, and I suspect she went willingly, but at that time she was betrothed to another man. If such sexual episodes are conducted discreetly, they do not attract much attention, but this one was far too flagrant to be ignored. Tanara's relatives were furious but found that for various reasons they could do little directly. Though feelings ran high at the time—the affair nearly precipitated a spear fight, the man went unpunished and now lives near the Warburton Ranges Mission. Katapi was particularly upset. Since Tanara is only Walanya's step-daughter, and since this couple does not appear to have any particularly close bond of affection such as exists between Mitapuyi and Nyurapaya, I suspect that Katapi may have had to talk Walanya into doing something to redress the grievance over Tanara. I further suspect that it was his decision to use sorcery and to call on Mitapuyi's abilities to this end.

Mitapuyi and his family had been encountered by an oil-exploration party at Tika-tika, a waterhole about forty miles from Partjar, in April 1965 and brought to the Warburton Ranges Mission. Katapi, her first husband, and their children were brought in by a Government patrol in September 1965, after being contacted in the same general area in April. For both families, this was the first direct contact with whites. They did not remain long in civilization, however. The death of Katapi's husband was an unsettling experience, which was followed, after Katapi's remarriage, by Tanara's involvement. In the conflicts that followed the latter event, it became apparent that there was little support for the newcomers. Also, the families were finding it hard to get enough food at the Mission. So in September 1966 the whole group left Warburton and walked back up to the country around Partjar and Tika-tika. At the Mission they had had few dealings with whites, since much of their time had been spent foraging in the desert country about forty miles to the north. By the time I joined them in the desert at Partjar, they had completely readapted to their traditional economy.

Now, in the seclusion of the sandhill country, Mitapuyi and Walanya appear to have decided to avenge by sorcery the injustices they encountered at the Mission. When I look at the exquisitely carved designs on the yirilmari being fashioned by Mitapuyi, I find it hard to believe that these two men consider this board a weapon as lethal as a gun. This attitude, incidentally, explains why desert Aborigines who have been given their first rifles sometimes fail to take ammunition with them. When they see an animal they raise the rifle and call out, "Pa! Pa!" The weapon seems to them to be another kind of magical pointing instrument. When they had seen whites using rifles they heard the report and saw the animal fall but they had explained this in terms of the magic they already understood. A few failures usually suffice to show them that something more is needed, and soon they learn about bullets.

Evening

Just before dark Mitapuyi and Walanya put the board back in its tree-cache and return to camp. During all this time the women have been grinding ngaṟu and kampuṟarpa. These tasks are nearly finished now, and Nyurapaya is impatient to make a new pair of sandals for herself. The taliwanti bark has been soaking in a wooden bowl ever since it was collected this morning, and it is now flexible enough to work with. Making a large loop by tying several strips of the bark together, Nyurapaya sits down inside the loop and anchors one end around her big toe and the other end behind her back. Then she draws the section in front of her together with a crosspiece of bark strip laced back and forth, until she has formed a sole pad about four inches wide and ten inches long. Finally, she cuts the loop which anchored it behind her, leaving two free strands, each about fifteen inches long, to serve as laces. When the sandals are worn, these laces are brought up from behind the heel through the long toe-loop, back around the ankle, and through the toe-loop again on the other side, where they are knotted under. It takes Nyurapaya only about half an hour to fashion a new pair of sandals. She is pleased to have new footwear and also with the tobacco I have given her for her old sandals.

The other women have been gathering some firewood and now build up the fires. It remains hot at night, the temperature hovering around 100 degrees, so the fires cannot be for warmth, and there is no more meat to be cooked. I am on the point of asking about this when one of the dogs, for no apparent reason, starts barking. Mitapuyi mutters, *"Mamu piṇi nyaratja tjinguṟu* [There are lots of night spirits out there perhaps]," and puts another piece of wood on his fire. I remember now having been told once that only dogs and sorcerers can see mamu and that fires will frighten them away. There are conflicting accounts of what a mamu can do, but in general there is agreement that they are spirits of the dead which hover in the darkness, sometimes making

Making bark sandals for
summer footwear.

a whistling noise, waiting to seize anyone out alone at night. They
are said to be cannibalistic. One of the most frequently voiced
reasons for keeping dogs is the warning they give of mamu. Besides mamu, any person abroad at night is assumed to have evil
intentions—perhaps to be intent on sorcery. Only the children
are much worried by the thought of a mamu lurking about; for

the adults, the dogs, the fires, and Mitapuyi's abilities as a sorcerer impart a strong feeling of security.

Conversation continues until about 7:30; then, one by one, children and adults start to drop off to sleep. Like women everywhere, Nyurapaya, Katapi, and Tjanangu keep on talking among themselves, long after everyone else is silent. Eventually, though, even their conversation stops. In the quiet, the only movements to be seen are flashes of brilliant meteors across the clear night sky.

Mitapuyi, even-tempered and a good kinsman; he is using his teeth to strip the bark from a mulga-wood staff to be fashioned into a digging-stick. His shy wife, Nyurapaya, wears a headdress of small eucalyptus nuts.

Katapi, strong-willed and competent.

Minmara, a man of outstanding good humor. Skilled in spear-making, he is sighting along a spearshaft to see if it is straight.

Tana, Katapi's eldest son, opening a ngaṛu *fruit with his sharp* pangara
stick.

Katapi's youngest son, Ngampakatju, collècting ngaṛu *fruit for his mother.*

The billabong at Partjaṛ, an oasis in the Gibson Desert. Beyond lie the Clutterbuck Hills.

Tjun, Mitapuyi's younger brother, wearing a falcon-feather headdress for a ceremony. (Left) The string headband is worn only by circumcised men.

Aborigine camps. (Above) *A summer camp at Mulyangiri, north of the Warburton Ranges. The shelters are built mainly to provide protection from the fierce heat of the sun.* (Below) *The winter camp of a Ngatatjara family, near the Warburton Ranges; its chief features are hearths and a brush windbreak.*

Betsy, encouraged by Nyurapaya, samples a wild berry called yawalyuru, *found near Tika-tika, a waterhole about 100 miles north of the Warburton Ranges Mission.*

A kangaroo roasting in live coals.

Katapi and Betsy discuss Ngampakatju's distended belly. The child's hair is almost as blond as Betsy's. (Below) Katapi cuffs Ngampakatju for unruly behavior—a rare occurrence among Aborigines, who indulge children to an extreme degree.

2

The Gibson Desert and
Its Early Explorers

Study a map of the continent of Australia, and you will observe one
vital fact which is having a tremendous influence there today.
Although the total area of Australia is nearly 3 million square
miles, the distance by air to any point in the center of the continent from any point along the coast is only 500 miles or a little
more. Among other things, this fact has meant that the remote interior deserts of Australia are far better known today from the air
than from travels on the ground. Aerial surveys have covered the
entire continent, and through them the first really accurate maps
of these deserts have been completed within the last ten years.
Landmarks like the Alfred and Marie Range which have tended

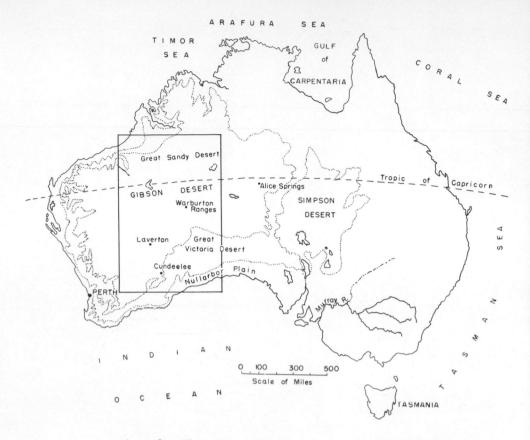

Australia. The area within the rectangle is the Gibson Desert,
home of the Ngatatjara and their kin; it is shown in larger scale
in the map on page 39.

to "wander" as much as a hundred miles out of position on different maps have finally been fixed by means of aerial photog-
raphy and mapping.

Aerial mapping, however, has made certain areas look better
known than they really are. This is particularly true of the Gibson Desert, a vast area between about 22 and 27 degrees south
latitude and 124 and 130 degrees east longitude in the state of
Western Australia. Ground parties have traversed this desert in
several places, and there are numerous graded tracks left by oil exploration teams and the Weapons Research Establishment (Woomera, South Australia). Much of the Gibson Desert lies along the
Woomera Rocket Range, and from 1958 through 1963 a network
of tracks was graded there for the purpose of recovering fallen

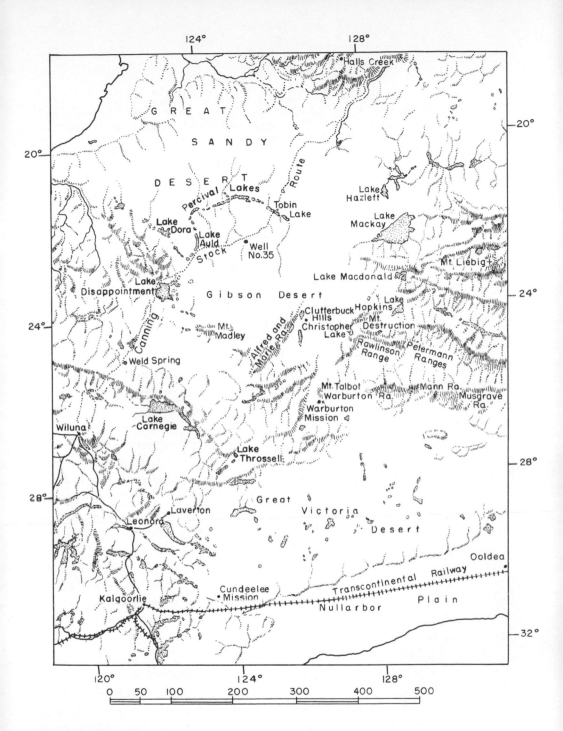

The Gibson Desert and adjoining regions of western Australia.

rockets. These roads, now much eroded, are known locally as the "Gunbarrel Highway," and they provide the best access into the area by land. In spite of these tracks, however, there are still huge blocks of country that have never been visited by Europeans.

Sand and Spinifex

In geographical terms, the Gibson Desert is not a well-defined entity. It forms part of a continuous series of deserts which make up most of the interior of Australia. To the north lies the Great Sandy Desert and to the south the Great Victoria Desert, both extremely arid and similar in character to the Gibson Desert. To the east there is more desert country, culminating in the Simpson Desert, the driest and most inhospitable of all. Boundaries between these deserts are arbitrary and serve only convenience in providing names one can refer to easily.

Most of the country can be classified as sandy desert, with parallel sand ridges, often many miles long, running in a generally northeast-southwest or east-west direction. These ridges are rarely over fifty feet high, with interdunal corridors of flat sand plain ranging from a few hundred yards to over a mile wide. Both dunes and sand plains have a cover of pale green spinifex grass which contrasts sharply with the red and pink tones of the sand. Spinifex is a desert-adapted plant with sharp spines. The spines can make walking across sandhill country extremely uncomfortable; small wonder that Ernest Giles, one of the early explorers of this region, referred with disgust to the plant as ". . . porcupine, triodia, spinifex, Festuca irritans, and everything-else-abominable, grass."[1] Throughout the Gibson Desert spinifex grows in clumps. The traveler today must make his way through this country by guiding his Land-Rover along the interdunal corridors, looking for openings and low spots along the sand ridges if he needs to make progress across the dunes. The driving is punctuated by sharp jolts caused by striking spinifex clumps. Crossing a sandhill requires a running headstart with gears set in four-wheel drive, while driver and passengers grimly hang on to avoid being buffeted against the roof of the cab. Several tries may be needed, with rest periods in between to allow overheated motors to cool (a good time, too, for that inevitable Australian institution, a cup of tea). The vista from the summit of the sandhill is not usually encouraging; as far as one can see, there are more sandhills, like stationary waves viewed from the shore of a petrified red sea.

The sandhill country is interrupted in places by large areas of what the Aborigines call *rira*—low, undulating knolls of reddish conglomerate, sometimes eroded in places into cliffs or "breakaways." In the driest areas these knolls have only a thin cover of spinifex or other grasses, but in some places these and the surrounding flats may be covered with mulga scrub of varying density. Although this vegetation has no actual thorns, it can be compared with thorn scrubs in other arid zones of the world. Dry, dead mulga trees usually fall over, exposing a radiating set of spikelike roots which resemble nothing so much as a large mace lying on its side. These stakes plagued early explorers by becoming embedded in the feet and legs of camels and horses, and for the modern traveler they can cause innumerable tire punctures and also penetrate a radiator or other vital bit of machinery. Dense mulga scrub is almost impenetrable for a vehicle, and an opening must be cleared through it beforehand, making slow progress for much hard work. Slivers of mulga wood in the flesh tend to fester rapidly, creating the additional problem of serious infections, which led Giles to suggest that mulga contained a poisonous substance.[2]

On most days, the country has a pale, washed-out appearance owing to the strong sunlight. But early in the morning and in the late afternoon and evening the contrasts of color and shadow can lead to scenes of surrealistic beauty. Groves of "desert oak" trees with their straight dark trunks and feathery needles stand out against the reddish sandhills. From time to time solitary desert kurrajong trees appear, their leaves a brilliant shade of green even in times of severe drought. And, most magnificent of all, there is the ghost gum with bark as white and smooth as an unmarked sheet of drawing paper.

The animals of the desert, like those in the rest of Australia, are shy and mainly nocturnal in their habits. Some kangaroos and euros may be seen during the day, but most of the smaller marsupials like the rabbit-eared bandicoot (*Thylacomys lagotis*), jerboa mouse (*Antechinomys spenceri*), and rock wallaby (*Petrogale pencillata*) emerge at night. The only large carnivore is the dingo, a variety of dog introduced to the Australian continent by man at least 3000 years ago.[3] Many dingoes run wild in the bush, although others live in a state of semidomestication with the Aborigines. Other introduced species include foxes, field mice, cats, camels, goats, and, of course, rabbits. All these animals have spread at the expense of native marsupial fauna. Today some species of small marsupials appear to be on the verge of extinction. Lizards are generally more common than mammals, the two largest being species of goanna. As a rule, the large marsupials frequent areas of mulga scrub, while lizards are more common in the spinifex vegetation of the sandhills and sand plains.

The desert is an ornithologist's delight. There is no mistaking the emu, which looks like an enormous feather-duster on stilts. These flightless birds are common wherever there is mulga cover, and they often travel in large groups during the day. They can run at speeds up to thirty miles per hour, but woe to the driver who tries to chase them in his Land-Rover. As the Mobil Road Guide of Western Australia coyly remarks: "A friendly word about emus—they tend to run directly ahead of you. Don't press them too closely or they'll foul your windscreen!" Emus are fascinating, but it is the smaller birds which provide most of the color and variety to the scene. Huge flocks of galahs (*Kakatoe roseicapilla*) dart around the waterholes, alternately flashing light gray and brilliant pink in the sun as they wheel overhead. Hordes of tiny finches with bright orange beaks and zebralike stripes along throat and breast (*Peophila guttata*) dash through the bushes around waterholes along with flights of green budgerigars (*Melopsittacus undulatus*), while a peregrine falcon or two sits patiently in a tree off to one side, and great wedge-tailed eagles (*Aquila audax*) swing overhead.

West of Alice Springs, the desert interior of Australia lacks any coherent system of drainage. Rainfall throughout most of the area averages less than 8 inches per year and tends to be highly irregular from one year to the next. Few rainfall figures are available for the region, but what there are suggest its erratic character. Rainfall in Alice Springs has ranged from 40.02 inches during the best recorded season (1920–21) to 1.77 inches during a fifteen-month drought.[4] In 1952–53 about 17 inches of rain fell at Phillip Creek, in Northern Territory, while only about 2 inches fell there in 1953–54.[5] Torrentially heavy local rains may occur, flooding creeks and creating temporary lakes in depressions between sandhills, while drought conditions prevail in neighboring regions. In the Warburton Ranges during the summer of 1966–67 about 8 inches of rain fell in the space of a couple of months, while the region about 150 miles to the northwest had almost no rain.

The fickle character of the rainfall in the Gibson Desert creates problems for the traveler. On the one extreme, there is the shortage of water. Giles evoked this continuous uncertainty over water: "To the traveler in such a wilderness, when he once turns his back upon a water, the ever-recurring question presents itself, of when and where shall I obtain more? The explorer is necessarily insatiable for water, no quantity can satisfy him, for he requires it always and in every place." [6]

On the other hand, there is the danger of becoming bogged after heavy rains. This is more of a problem today, with motor vehicles, than it was in Giles' day, but it sometimes happened then, too. Scattered through the desert are numerous large and small dry lakebeds. The largest of these are Lake Carnegie and Lake Disappointment on the west, Lake Throssel and Lake Yeo to the south, Lakes Hopkins, Macdonald, Mackay, and Hazlett on the northeast, and the Percival Lakes on the north. All these are usually dry, with a firm bed of mud and salt, but even a small amount of rain can transform a lakebed into quagmire. After heavy rains these lakes will hold water, though it is usually salty and undrinkable. In April 1967, following a period of unusually heavy rains, I visited the Percival Lakes in the company of a Woomera Rocket Range patrol. The sight which awaited us was a vast sheet of saline water, perhaps 70 or 80 miles long, about 3 miles wide, and about 6 inches deep, looking like an inland sea set in the midst of sandhills and spinifex.

The hardships presented by the Gibson Desert are not the

overwhelming dramatic sort faced by Himalayan climbers, polar explorers, or visitors to the Amazon Basin or the Sahara. Aside from the dingo (which never attacks human beings), there are no large carnivores in Australia to threaten one's sense of security in the bush, but there are hordes of smaller pests. Flies abound, particularly after rains. Seeking moisture and nutrients, they crawl into eyes, ears, nostrils, and mouth with exasperating persistence. At night there are numerous ants of assorted sizes. Whenever the desert Aborigines want to communicate the idea of "a lot" or "very many" of something, their comment, aptly enough, is *"minga pinpa* [like ants]." But these creatures are harmless compared to the venomous red-back spiders, the centipedes, the scorpions, or the dreaded *liru* or mulga snake (*Demansia textilis*). Eye and skin ailments caused by bacteria carried by dust and flies are a common hazard, as are extremes of temperature. Summer temperatures averaging around 120 in the shade are not unusual, and winter nighttime temperatures may creep below freezing.

The Explorers

In 1873–74 the desert region west of Alice Springs received its first European visitors. Four explorers almost simultaneously converged on the area in search of potential grazing lands and, above all, a practical overland route for bringing livestock across the continent for export.[7] All four reacted in the same way to this country, regarding it as inhospitable and hazardous to cross. Their journals are filled mainly with accounts of the dangers posed by shortage of water and food and the difficulties of traversing vast distances, as well as endless annoyances of the "pinprick" variety posed by flies, ants, infections, dust, glare, heat, and cold. None of these men had a comfortable or rewarding time. All met with repeated hardship and frustration. Their expeditions were all failures in the sense that they did not find the overland stock route they sought. At the end of their travels, they were all relieved to be out of the desert and back in civilization.

In September 1874, all four explorers were in the field, and, of the four, three were in trouble. Although they traveled independently, each was aware that the others were actively exploring the same general area. Colonel Philip Egerton-Warburton was the first to depart for the interior, leaving Adelaide on September 21, 1872, and arriving in Alice Springs three months later. Warburton's party was well equipped with provisions and depended entirely on camels for transport. But fear of becoming bogged by torrential summer rains caused Warburton to delay his departure from Alice Springs until April 15, 1873. The party was large, with seven members (four whites, two Afghan camel-drivers, and an Aborigine). The expedition started well, as Warburton traversed the north side of the Macdonnell Range, but ran into difficulties farther west. Owing to an eclipse of the moon which took him by surprise, Warburton's navigation was in error for nearly the entire trip, causing him to miss several key waterholes.

The expedition was halted for forty-two days at one waterhole while Warburton and the others scouted in different directions in search of other water sources. The delay reduced their precious supplies, and before long it was apparent that they had attempted this difficult crossing in a drought year. To make things worse, four of their best camels escaped into the desert. From time to time they captured an Aborigine whom they forced to lead them to a waterhole. At one time they spotted smoke rising from an Aboriginal camp. The Aborigines ran off when they approached, and the expedition took over the waterhole. Four more camels died, and the party, short of food by this time, was forced to eat the animals:

"We jerked our camel meat as well as we could, but it is very poor food; the animal was old and quite worn out. The travelling these dark nights over such bad ground as these sandridges is very slow." [8]

Because of the preoccupation with food and water and the extreme heat (which forced the party to travel at night), the expedition recorded little useful information about the country it passed through or about the native inhabitants. By September 1873, the party's supplies were nearly gone, and the search for water determined the route of travel. As a result, the expedition veered far to the north and then to the southwest, while the ordeal stretched on day after day. The only food came from camels which were periodically slaughtered and from whatever small game the party chanced upon. By November 12, their plight was so serious that Warburton himself despaired of ever reaching the Oakover River, their only hope of relief:

"My party at least are now in such a state that, unless it please God to save us, we cannot live more than twenty-four hours. We are at our last drop of water, and the smallest bit of dried meat chokes me. . . . The country is terrible. I do not believe men ever traversed so vast an extent of continuous desert." [9]

This dire prediction was premature, however, for the party held on until it reached a tributary of the Oakover River on December 4. Here their fortunes improved rapidly, and they were met by a relief party from the De Grey station, a homestead not far away. All the members of the expedition survived, but it had been a close call with little in the way of useful results to show for all the misery and toil.

Using camels and a cart, William C. Gosse set out from Alice Springs on April 21, 1873, for the desert shortly after Warburton but reached unexplored territory at about the same time. His route carried him far to the south of Warburton's track, in the direction of Ayers Rock and Mount Olga. Gosse was the first European to examine these remarkable monolithic formations. Like Warburton's, his party was large and well equipped. There were nine men on the expedition, including five whites, three Afghan camelteers, and an Aborigine boy. The group was speeded on its way by good rains.

Continuing in a southerly direction, Gosse reached the Mann and Tomkinson ranges, where he turned west into less well-watered country. By mid-September his expedition was camped in the Cavanagh Range, and the prospect of finding water was becoming uncertain. A reconnaissance farther west reached the Townshend Range, but at that point Gosse decided that the risks of continuing were too great. The party turned back on September 22 and returned without incident.

Gosse had greater success in a short time than any of the other explorers who entered this area. It is easy to be attracted by the endurance of Warburton and that of Ernest Giles in the face of tremendous hardships, in much the same way as we empathize with the sufferings of men like Scott and Shackleton in the Antarctic, and in this light, Gosse's achievement seems almost too easy. He found the country hostile and unrewarding, so he turned back rather than face the trials he knew lay ahead. Gosse was the first European to penetrate this region, and he named most of the important landmarks from the Mann Range to the Townshend Range. His expedition was well planned, and he showed good judgment in turning back when he did. The ordeal faced by Giles shortly afterward proved Gosse right.

Ernest Giles was one of the most colorful figures in the history of exploration in Australia. His journals are filled with flowery and uninformative prose which delighted the romantics of the Victorian era. He was a man of great personal courage and strength, but his judgment about practical matters was not always good. He chose to use horses instead of camels, and he made an unfortunate choice for a companion in Alfred Gibson. Gibson comes off rather badly in Giles' journals as a man who never bathed and who lacked both intelligence and experience. Giles preferred to travel light, with a small party (the second-in-command, W. H. Tietkens, Gibson, and a youngster named Jimmy Andrews) carrying a minimum of equipment. His efforts were financed by Baron Ferdinand von Mueller, a distinguished botanist of German extraction who was a patron of Australian exploration. The Baron's influence accounts for the repertory of Germanic names which Giles applied to landmarks he discovered.

In 1872 Giles made a short exploration into the region around Lake Amadeus, during which he caught a glimpse of Mount Olga but failed to penetrate deeply into the desert. Upon his return, Giles learned of the attempts being undertaken by Warburton and Gosse. He returned to Victoria and hurriedly organized another expedition with the aim of going farther into the desert and perhaps crossing the continent. Plunging into the same area he had been in earlier, he and his three companions were disappointed to discover tracks left only a short while earlier by Gosse's cart. They had hoped to be the first Europeans to visit this region. Nevertheless, they pressed on, little realizing that Gosse was on the verge of turning back. At the end of September Gosse and Giles, going in opposite directions, passed within a few miles of each other without realizing it.

By this time Giles was already experiencing the same difficulties which had caused Gosse to retreat. But Giles kept going west. By November 1873, he was camped in the Cavanagh Range, very near the spot where Gosse had camped, and he had seen a second set of Gosse's cart tracks close upon the first, so he knew Gosse had started back to civilization. Giles used this place as a base camp and named it Fort Mueller in honor of his patron. During December Giles reconnoitered to a point just west of the Warburton Ranges (named by him on this occasion) but turned back for lack of water. On January 14, 1874, Giles and his companions were attacked by a party of Aborigines at Fort Mueller. Giles offered no explanation for the incident. There was much commotion and spears were thrown at the camp, but the Aborigines were soon driven off by a few shots fired in their midst. There is no mention of anyone's being hurt or killed.

From this area, Giles caught a glimpse of another high range in the distance to the north. Forced to abandon his westward route through lack of water, he turned north. After crossing a difficult belt of sandhill country, the party reached a range of high mountains of brilliant red and yellow rock. This Giles named the Rawlinson Range, and he traversed it to the west, finding deep gorges and large waterholes along the way. At the western end of the range he established another base camp which he called Circus Water, and it was from here that he planned another attempt to proceed west across the continent.

The Rawlinson Range and the Petermann Range to the east were among Giles' most important discoveries on this occasion. The scenery in these mountains is dramatic, second only to Ayers Rock and Mount Olga, with brilliant shades of red and purple emerging at sunrise and sunset. With his characteristic penchant for picturesque names, Giles bestowed a series of romantic labels on the gorges and passes he encountered there: the Gorge of Tarns, the Pass of the Abencerrages, Desolation Glen, Ruined Rampart, the Schwerin Mural Crescent, and Mount Destruction (so named because the trek to this big solitary peak cost him the lives of four horses).

Although the expedition found temporary relief in these ranges from the rigors of the sandhill country, Giles' effort to push on to the west proved disastrous. On April 21, 1874, Giles and Gibson departed from Circus Water with two horses to investigate the country to the west. They traveled about one hundred miles, making their way along corridors between the high sandhills that cover this region, until they came within sight of a long row of hills which Giles named the Alfred and Marie Range. At this point, Gibson's horse collapsed, and the two men had to turn back. Giles instructed Gibson to continue back to Circus Water with the remaining horse while he followed alone on foot. Gibson was to have returned with fresh horses in a few days, but on his way he lost sight of the track they had left and disappeared without a trace. Meanwhile, Giles made his way back by night to conserve moisture, and nine days after separating from Gibson he arrived at the waterhole.

Later Giles and his party made a diligent but fruitless search for Gibson. Afterward, Giles named the area Gibson's Desert ". . . after the first white victim to its horrors." [10] In terms of pure physical endurance, Giles' lonely trek through the Gibson Desert (as it is now called) back to the Rawlinson Range must surely stand as a high point in the history of Australian exploration. To the obvious agonies of extreme thirst and exhaustion were added the sublime tortures of spinifex spines and ants:

"Generally speaking, whenever I saw a shady desert oak-tree there was an enormous bulldog ants' nest under it, and I was prevented from sitting in its shade. On what I thought was the 27th I almost gave up the thought of walking any further, for the exertion of this dreadful region, where the triodia was almost as high as myself, and thick as it could grow, was quite overpowering, and being starved, I felt quite light-headed. After sitting down, on every occasion when I tried to get up again, my head would swim round, and I would fall down oblivious for some time. Being in a chronic state of burning thirst, my general plight was dreadful in the extreme. A bare and level sandy waste would have been Paradise to walk over compared to this. My arms, legs, thighs, both before and behind, were so punctured with spines, it was agony only to exist; the slightest movement and in went more spines, where they broke off in the clothes and flesh, causing the whole of the body that was punctured to gather into minute pustules which were continually growing and bursting." [11]

Giles and the remainder of his party made their way back along the Rawlinson and Petermann ranges to Mount Olga, and thence as quickly as they could back to Adelaide. Aside from the discovery of these great central ranges, the expedition had been a failure. In 1875–76, Giles made another expedition across Australia, this time from west to east. On this occasion he used camels for transport, and the trip was speedy and relatively uneventful. He passed through the Gibson Desert again, but it was winter then and far cooler than it had been on his previous visit. When he saw the Alfred and Marie Range again, Giles realized the total futility of his earlier attempt to reach and move beyond this group of hills:

"The first sight of these ranges from the east, had cost my former horse expedition into this region so dear. I could not help believing that the guiding hand of a gracious Providence had upon that occasion prevented me from obtaining my heart's desire to reach them; for had I done so, I know now, having proved what kind of country lay beyond, that neither I nor any of my former party would ever have returned." [12]

In 1874 John Forrest made the first successful west-to-east crossing of the continent, with his brother, Alexander, as second-in-command. The party consisted of six whites and two Aborigines, with twenty horses for packing supplies and riding. Forrest would have preferred to use camels, but there were none available in Western Australia at that time. They left Perth on March 18, 1874, and progressed rapidly to the headwaters of the Murchison River, from which they set out to cross the Gibson Desert. On June 2 they reached a fine cluster of freshwater seepages which they named Weld Spring in honor of the Governor of Western Australia at the time. The party was attacked by Aborigines at this place, and at least one Aborigine was hit by rifle fire. The discovery of Weld Spring was a stroke of luck for the explorers, for it proved to be an oasis where they could rest and prepare for their dash to the east. Game was plentiful, and the party remained there for seventeen days. Forrest's explorations were notable for their strict discipline, with regular watches and a careful routine of scouting ahead for water. Much as one may admire Giles for his personal courage and endurance, there is no doubt that he might have been spared much agony, including the loss of his companion Gibson, if he had set up a regular routine like Forrest's and kept to it. Forrest had luck, too, for on June 22, when the party was well out in the desert, a fresh-water lake was sighted. The discovery of this lake, which Forrest named Lake Augustus, enabled the explorers to continue eastward instead of turning back to Weld Spring as they had been on the verge of doing. As they proceeded, each time they were about to turn back for lack of water, a new spring or water-hole was found and they could go on. Through a combination of luck and careful planning, the expedition sighted the Warburton Ranges by July 30 and, after a week-long reconnaissance, found water there, along with horse tracks and other signs left by Giles eight months earlier. Here again, they would have been forced to go back had water not been found when it was. The remainder of the journey was uneventful, as Forrest and his party moved eastward in the tracks of Giles and Gosse, and they soon reached civilization.

Forrest's and Giles' exploits concluded the first wave of exploration in this region. There were others who came later— W. W. Mills in 1883, David Lindsay and L. A. Wells in 1891, David Carnegie and Wells in 1896, and Frank Hann in 1903 and 1906–1907. They too experienced a multitude of dangers and discomforts and remarked in their journals on the hostility of the country they passed through. There also were some fatalities. Two members of Wells' 1896 exploring party (one the leader's cousin) separated from the others, intending to rejoin them at Joanna Springs, a waterhole discovered by Warburton. But the longitude given by Warburton for the waterhole was wrong, and the two men lost their way in the sandhills and perished. The descriptions of the country given by these later explorers are useful but serve mainly to reinforce the impressions of the discoverers. These impressions of the Gibson Desert region as a dangerous and uninhabitable place persist today among white Australians, and the usual reaction to my questions about the country was that it is "bloody awful."

It was not until 1906–1907 that an explorer made any serious effort to meet the Aborigines in this region and learn from them about the locations of waterholes. This explorer was A. W. Canning, who traveled from Wiluna northeastward to Halls Creek surveying a stock route (later known in his honor as the Canning Stock Route) across the western end of the Gibson Desert. The trek extended over 800 miles, and there is no question that the knowledge passed on to Canning by the local Aborigines gave him a definite advantage in his travels. It has been many years since the stock route Canning pioneered has seen any use (sea shipment of livestock is easier now), but occasional travelers to remote wells along the old route can still see the gaunt timbers and rusted pulleys that once drew water for thirsty camels, cattle, and their drovers.

Among all the early explorers of this region only Canning and Richard Helms,[13] a member of the Elder Exploring Expedition of 1891 (the same one that included Lindsay and Wells), did much to develop contacts with the Aborigines. Some, like Warburton and Carnegie, exploited these people in a brutal manner which fostered their distrust. Carnegie once actually tied an Aborigine to his camel-saddle and fed him salted meat to force him to lead his expedition to water. Naturally the Aborigines were apprehensive about these strange-looking newcomers. The explorers also put a strain on the Aborigines' economy without giving anything in return. Imagine the chagrin of a family of Aborigines on finding its waterholes drunk dry by a herd of thirsty camels. Much of the disdain shown by the explorers for the Aborigines can be attributed to the widespread Victorian-era notion of the inferiority of most native peoples in contrast to Europeans. The early explorers (Giles, Gosse, Warburton, and Forrest) were curious about the Aborigines, but not enough so to attempt any communication with them. Instead, they made offhand judgments based more on conjecture than on observation. For example, Giles suggested that the Aborigines living around the Rawlinson Range were cannibals,[14] and also that human sacrifice was practiced by these same natives at a spot near Gill's Pinnacle at the east end of the range.[15] Both suggestions were untrue, outgrowths of Giles' vivid imagination.

Had early explorers attempted to learn the language of the Aborigines and observed their behavior more closely, their trips would have been far less harrowing. They might have felt more at home in this country, and they would certainly have been less pressed for food and, above all, for water.

To the Aborigines the desert is home. Though they are well aware of its dangers, they derive a satisfaction from their close association with the country which it is hard for an outsider to grasp. The early explorers were in a unique position, for they were the first whites to meet these people and could observe them under conditions completely unaffected by European culture, but none of the explorers seems to have had any comprehension of the Aborigines' ties to their country. Yet to appreciate this sense of belonging to the land is to begin to understand the Aborigines, a people whose culture is truly different from ours. And to understand them is perhaps to understand ourselves, too, by contrast.

Who Are the Desert Aborigines?

Discussion of the Australian Aborigines, even more than that of native peoples in other parts of the world, seems to conjure up such pejorative terms as primitive, childlike, Stone Age, savage. An early observer commented about the Australian and Tasmanian Aborigines: "In respect of culture they stood at an undisputably lower plane than any people now on the face of the earth, or known to have existed for many thousands of years past." [1] Another remarked on "the low position of the Australian savage in the scale of the human species." [2]

One reason for the wide acceptance of views of this kind was historical coincidence. The Australian scholars W. Baldwin Spencer and F. J. Gillen published the first detailed and reliable account of an Australian desert tribe, the Arunta (or Aranda, as they are called by some), in 1899,[3] a few decades after scholars in Europe first discovered and recognized the remains of Paleolithic man. The awareness of Neanderthal man and of the brilliant cave art left later by men of the European Upper Paleolithic had led to speculation. How did these ancient people live? To what extent did they resemble modern man? What about their social life and religion? With questions like these, scholars turned enthusiastically to descriptions of the Arunta and other Aborigines in search of answers.

From these inquiries there arose a point of view. The Australian Aborigines (particularly desert people like the Arunta) were thought to be direct survivals of the kind of Stone Age culture represented by Neanderthal man.[4] One of the foremost scholars to echo these sentiments was Dr. Sigmund Freud, who in the first chapter of his psychological-anthropological treatise, *Totem and Taboo* (1918), declared: ". . . there are people whom we still consider more closely related to primitive man than to ourselves, in whom we therefore recognize the direct descendants and representatives of earlier man. . . . I am choosing for this comparison those tribes which have been described by ethnographists as being most backward and wretched: the aborigines of the youngest continent, namely Australia, whose fauna has also preserved for us so much that is archaic and no longer to be found elsewhere."

This interpretation still haunts popular ideas about Aborigines, even though it has been discarded by most scholars.

Ancient Man in Australia

Like all peoples, the Aborigines have a history. Because they have not developed any form of writing, they lack a written history, and their mythology and oral traditions are not particularly helpful in this regard. Until recently one could only speculate about Aboriginal history, following tantalizing but uncertain lines of evidence. However, in 1929, two Australian scholars, Herbert M. Hale and Norman B. Tindale of the South Australian

Museum, introduced fresh evidence of a different kind. In the Murray River Valley in South Australia, at a place called Devon Downs, they carried out archaeological excavations which revealed a sequence of ancient cultures leading up to the historic Aborigines of the region.[5] This was an important step, for archaeological excavation provides the best available means of finding out about the history of nonliterate peoples.

During the last twenty years such excavations have been begun in Australia on a large scale. Stratified archaeological sites have been discovered in every state of Australia, including Tasmania, and work is continuing in all these areas. Though much remains to be done, this research has already led to definite and important results. We now know that man has been in Australia for at least 20,000 years.[6] It seems fairly certain that at all times and in all parts of Australia the Aborigines depended for their livelihood on hunting game and foraging for wild plant foods. There is no evidence that agriculture ever appeared, or was likely to, before the arrival of Europeans. But several excavations have uncovered important changes in technology. At some sites, including Kenniff Cave in Queensland, Puntutjarpa Rockshelter in the Warburton Ranges of Western Australia, and Nawamoyn, Tyimede, and Malangangerr rockshelters near the coast of Arnhem Land, Northern Territory, there is evidence for early industries based on the manufacture of fairly large stone flakes, probably used as scrapers. In all these sites the flakes were accompanied by a distinctive type of steep-sided stone cores which many Australian archaeologists have called "horsehoofs" because of their hooflike shape. These horsehoof cores may also have been used as scrapers. One Australian archaeologist, Dr. D. J. Mulvaney, has inferred from their large size that tools like these were held directly in the hand by their users rather than being hafted to a wood or bone handle.[7] Impressed by the remarkable similarities of stone tools from the lower levels of these widely scattered sites, one archaeologist has half-jokingly referred to this as the "bottomoid" industry of Australia. Axheads of ground stone have also been discovered from the bottom levels of the Arnhem Land rockshelters, associated with horsehoofs and large flake tools. Some of these stone axheads, however, have definite grooves, indicating that they were attached to handles of some kind.[8]

Evidence from Kenniff Cave and other archaeological sites shows a change toward the hafting of chipped-stone tools, which culminates in the appearance of small, elegantly made microliths. The earliest probable occurrence of these is from about 6700 years ago at Puntutjarpa Rockshelter,[9] with those in the eastern states first appearing, on present evidence, about 1000 years later. These assemblages include a variety of distinctive forms, such as crescent-shaped flakes ("lunates") and asymmetrical crescents ("Bondi points"), as well as tiny discoidal scrapers and, in parts of southeastern Australia, small unifacially flaked points ("pirri points"). This shift from hand-held to hafted tools is an important change in the history of ancient Aboriginal technology and the hafting is clearly of a different kind from that represented by the early ground-stone axheads from Arnhem Land. So well made are many of these microliths that they have an almost jewel-like quality.

Despite this evidence for change, there is also a strong element of continuity in the overall history of Aboriginal stone technology. Throughout the sequence at Puntutjarpa Rockshelter in Western Australia, large flake tools continued in use at the same time that microliths were in vogue. In other words, microliths and other small hafted tools became popular but never entirely replaced hand-held stone tools. This situation persists even up to the present. The Aborigines living in the desert around the Warburton Ranges no longer make microliths, but they do make stone tools which appear to be the direct descendants of some of the microliths and are hafted to wooden handles. At the same time they also use several kinds of hand-held stone tools.[10]

Thus present evidence suggests that the Aborigines have a basically uninterrupted history. There are no signs of any sharp breaks in the economy and technology, no indications that outsiders might have disrupted local patterns of development. Microlithic tools similar in appearance to some of the Australian varieties have been found widely distributed in Upper Paleolithic

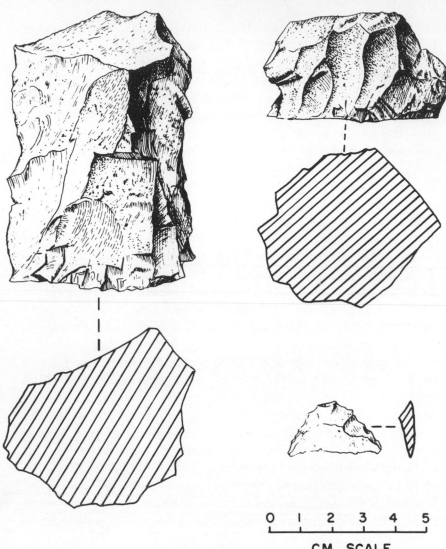

Artifacts from excavations at Puntutjarpa Rockshelter, near the Warburton Ranges. (*Above*) "Horsehoof" cores from lower levels; similar artifacts are known from even earlier sites in other parts of Australia. (*Lower right*) A "lunate," crescent-shaped tool found with others of the same type at Puntutjarpa Rockshelter.

and later cultures of Europe, and in Africa and India as well. Perhaps the manufacture of these tools spread to Australia from Asia, or perhaps the ancient Aborigines invented it independently. At this time it is impossible to decide which explanation is correct, but one thing is certain: the present-day Australian Aborigines cannot be cultural survivals of the Lower Paleolithic peoples of Europe, as represented by Neanderthal man. Enough technological changes have occurred in the last 20,000 years to show that they have a history of their own and cannot be considered as a mere "survival" or relic culture. Any Australian resemblances to the culture of Neanderthal man would appear to result from analogy rather than historical connection.

Brown Skins and Blond Hair

Some early scholars also thought that the Australian Aborigines looked like Neanderthal man.[11] From my own experience I know that it is easy to form this impression when first meeting a group of Aborigines. Many have massive brow ridges, a Neanderthal-like characteristic. Most reconstructions of Neanderthal man show him with a dark skin and a broad nose, both also features commonly met with among Aborigines. But, just as with Aboriginal culture, these similarities are more apparent than real.

Recent studies of the physical characteristics of Australian Aborigines have confirmed the statement by American anthropologist Sherwood L. Washburn: ". . . the aboriginal Australian is definitely a modern man and lacks the peculiarities of the face and limb bone which characterize ancient man [including Neanderthal]."[12]

This being true, can we say that the Aborigines represent a distinct race? Some scholars think so and designate them as the Australoid race.[13] The basis for this classification lies in a series of physical features which most Aborigines, including the desert people, share and which serve to distinguish them from other groups of man. These include the dark skin pigmentation, broad noses, and heavy brow ridges mentioned before, along with plentiful body and facial hair, thick skullcap (sometimes slightly keel-shaped on top), slender arms, legs, and buttocks, and sometimes prognathic jaws (that is, jaws which project forward in the region of the mouth). It has also been suggested that these features, which, taken together, identify the Australoid race, are found in areas of the world outside Australia, for example, among the Veddas of Ceylon, the Sakai of the Malay region, and among some tribes of New Guinea and India.[14]

However, as Washburn goes on to say, ". . . racial classification is a *simple sampling system* which allows a student to become familiar with the superficial physical characters of two billion people in a remarkably short period of time." [15]

Note the use of the word "superficial." The point is that there are complexities which racial classifications do not adequately describe. For example, the Aborigines show notable variations in degree of pigmentation and in stature, as well as in hair color and form. Many people are surprised to learn that some desert Aborigines, particularly women and children, have brilliant blond hair. While most Aborigines have long, straight hair, I have met several individuals with markedly curly hair. Such "typical" features as brow ridges and nose form also vary, and a close acquaintance with these people leads inevitably to the conclusion that the concept of a uniform Australoid race is an extreme generalization. It depends entirely on outward appearances.

Trying to get away from such a heavy dependence on outward physical features, anthropologists in Australia, following research trends in other parts of the world, have taken an interest in genetics, and have turned to the genetics of blood-group systems as the best way of finding out about the mixing or isolation of populations. These studies of populations in the Gibson Desert and adjacent areas have furnished some startling results. Australian biologist Robert L. Kirk recently observed that the Aborigines of the Gibson, Victoria, and Great Sandy deserts have been reproductively isolated for a long period of time and have been subject to selective pressures in an unusually harsh environment throughout that time. He notes that this population possesses the highest frequency of A_1 gene in the ABO blood

group system anywhere in Australia, as well as the highest fre-
quencies on the continent for at least two other blood-factors.
He also points out that this region ". . . has yielded the only
known example in the world of a person without any detectable
Rh antigen." [16] These findings reinforce the general impressions
created by the archaeological evidence that the desert Aborigines
have a long history coupled with a relatively high degree of isolation from the rest of the world. Both physically and culturally
they have changed and adapted in their own ways and cannot be
simply dismissed as static survivals.

The physical adaptations shown by the desert Aborigines
go beyond genetic and racial characteristics. Many of their most
distinctive physical attributes are acquired during the individual's lifetime of coping with a nomadic life in the desert. Travelers to this region have remarked on the Aborigines' ability to
sit cross-legged on the ground for hours on end. This is the usual
way for the men to sit, and the women sometimes sit this way
too, alternating with a kind of collapsed kneeling position in
which the legs are pulled together under the thighs. Most Europeans and Americans find either of the positions uncomfortable
even for a short time, but for the Aborigines they are relaxing.
Their ability to "bend" comfortably in these ways is a result of a
lifetime of practice. Conversely, Aborigine children who have
just come out of the desert sometimes are miserable for weeks
while trying to adjust to sitting on chairs in government or mission
schools.

One hot day after we had been walking in the desert for
hours, I handed my Aborigine companion a nearly full two-gallon
waterbag. Although he had not complained of being thirsty or
asked me for water, he proceeded to drink it all, right then and
there. This ability to eat and drink in prodigious amounts at one
sitting (or gulp) has been noted many times among the Aborigines. Dr. H. H. Finlayson, Australian zoologist and traveler to this
region in the early 1930s, noted that ". . . when the opportunity
comes of slaking their thirst, they [the Aborigines] perform feats
of swilling far beyond any white man's capacity." [17] Eating and
drinking in this gargantuan manner must be looked upon as an
adaptation to the uncertainties of desert living. Lacking any

means of storing meat or carrying large quantities of water, these people can go for long periods without food or water, while making the most of opportunities to eat and drink when they arise.

Until they settle in close contact with whites, the Aborigines have remarkably healthy teeth. Dental caries is rare, and teeth are used for a wide variety of chores besides eating. Men often perform pressure-flaking on stone tools with their teeth. They also strip bark from wooden sticks and branches with their teeth, and on several occasions I have watched men clamp their teeth around a wooden spearshaft while bending and rebending it to make it straight. It is common to see a man take dried emu or kangaroo sinew and chew on it for a while, like a piece of gum, to make it moist and elastic. The moistened sinew is used to bind and haft certain items like spear-barbs and spearthrower hooks. As the sinew dries it shrinks, making the binding even tighter. A closer look reveals that these people have flat teeth—that is, teeth on which the crowns have been worn flat. This is due mainly to the tough and gritty foods they consume, and the condition appears to cause no pain or discomfort. Their jaw muscles are also strong, mainly because of the tough, undercooked meat they consume, making it possible for them to apply their teeth to these tasks with a strong, viselike bite.

Except in the extreme heat of summer, the desert Aborigines go barefoot. Their feet develop thickly callused soles for protection against sharp stones and thorns. A man can walk for hours with a collection of small thorns stuck into the bottom of his foot, not feeling a thing and picking the thorns out only at the end of his journey. Large thorns, however, are pulled out immediately. Sometimes lateral cracks develop in the sole, and a thorn in one of these deep cracks can cause excruciating pain. But otherwise such thickened soles are a boon.

Similar physical adaptations have been reported for other hunting and gathering peoples such as the Eskimo, Bushmen, Andaman Islanders, Congo Pygmies, and several North American Indian societies. Such adaptations show how readily human physique can adjust to a variety of environments and point to an easy acceptance of conditions which most Europeans and Americans would soon find intolerable. The Aborigines are barely conscious of this acceptance until the presence of a *walypala* ("whitefella") shows them the difficulties *he* faces in adjusting to their routine. There would always be some discreet laughter from the Aborigines whenever my knees popped as I sat down to join them in the shade, followed by solicitous remarks on my "condition," such as *"Nyuntuku muṭi pikatjara tjinguṛu* [Your knee is ill, perhaps]?"

A Manner of Speaking

The Aborigines of the Gibson Desert call their language Pitjantjara (or sometimes Pitjantjatjara)—"those having the word *pitja* [come]"—when speaking of it generally, but they also distinguish numerous dialects which they name with reference to the groups of people who speak them. These dialect-names are more important than any territorial or tribal identifications in denoting groups of people. The dialect spoken around the Warburton Ranges encompasses a large group of people who are called Ngatatjara—"those having the word *nga:tja* [this]," while people from the desert area north of the Rawlinson Range speak several dialects lumped loosely under the heading "Pintupi." In some cases the number of speakers of a particular dialect is very small. I know of only a few families, totaling around thirty people (including Mitapuyi and the others at Partjar), that converse in the dialect called Nyatunyatjara—"those having the word *nyatunya* [kangaroo]." The speakers of this restricted dialect forage over a large area of sandhill and mulga country from an area west of the Rawlinson Range through the Clutterbuck Hills and the Alfred and Marie Range to a region near a waterhole called Taltiwara, a total of roughly 150 miles from east to west.

All these dialects appear to be part of a mutually intelligible series running all the way from Ooldea in South Australia to the Kimberley region of Western Australia and across from Oodnadatta in South Australia to Meekatharra in Western Australia.[18] Thus this language encompasses a vast and irregular area about

900 miles from north to south and 1100 miles from east to west. The terms and phrases used in this book and listed in the glossary and pronunciation guide all derive from the Ngatatjara dialect.

One authority estimates the present population of Western Desert Aborigines (all Pitjantjara speakers) at between approximately 2000 and 3200 and he suggests that between 10,000 and 18,000 persons may have inhabited this region before European contact.[19] This is a rough estimate at best, but it gives some idea of the scale of the overall population and makes it readily apparent that at the time of European contact the density of Aboriginal population in the desert was extremely low—on an order of perhaps one person for every 35 to 40 square miles.[20] With these figures in mind, the marked linguistic uniformity of these people over such a vast area assumes a new importance. It suggests that, despite the distances involved and the physical and archaeological evidence that they have lived in the desert in comparative isolation for thousands of years, they have found ways to maintain enough regular contact among themselves to prevent their dialects from changing into mutually unintelligible languages.

Learning to Speak Ngatatjara

The following section is intended mainly for people who enjoy doing crossword puzzles, anagrams, and other word games. Here I have tried to present some of the essential characteristics of this dialect by way of showing how it feels to confront an unusual new language and struggle with it. Those who would rather not be burdened with linguistic detail should proceed directly to the next chapter.

Under normal conditions Aborigines speak rapidly, certainly faster than English is spoken and, indeed, than any other language I have heard. Stress always occurs on the first syllable of any word—something which English-speakers often find difficult when first learning an Aboriginal language. To facilitate rapid speech, people, particularly the women, are prone to speaking continuously as they breathe, both on the in- and the out-breaths. This is a real feat, and I have never known a non-native speaker who could master it. Word order in sentences is relatively unimportant, but suffixing is essential and sometimes complex. Compared to English and the Romance languages, the Aboriginal language is a paragon of consistency. There are only a few irregular verbs. An example of simple suffixing is the sentence:

ngayu lu		*wangka*	*nintiri*	*ngkutjaku*
I		language	learn	would like
	(subject suffix)		(verb stem)	(suffix expressing desire)

or "I would like to learn the language."

One factor which complicates things for the learner is the tendency of native speakers to make contractions of commonly used forms. Instead of saying:

ngayu lu		*nyuntu nya*		*nintil*	*ku*
I		you		give	will
	(subject suffix)		(object suffix)	(verb stem)	(future suffix)

or "I will give it to you," the chances are that the speaker will simply say: "*Nintilkunanta.*" (The suffix *-na* replaces the first person subject, and the suffix *-nta* the second person object.) It takes a while to learn these additional suffixes (since, of course, it has already taken a while to learn the forms they replace), and I was never very good at this. But I tried, and so did my wife, who definitely did better than I. The Aborigines are a courteous people who sympathize with anyone willing to make the effort to learn their language, so I was encouraged to practice some of the more complex forms. I would learn a new form such as nintilkunanta, then proceed to the Aborigines' camp and spring it on them in the course of my work. There would be a pause, then a comment of good-humored and exaggerated awe: "*Lara nintipuka* [Wow, it's a learned man]!" Then they would resume their rapid conversation, often as not leaving me far behind.

Much of the vocabulary consists of words with specialized or local meanings, such as the names for certain kinds of plants, artifacts, or geographic features, which, of course, cannot be translated easily into English, since no strict equivalents exist in the English-speaking world. For instance, *kalpaṛi* is a plant of which the seeds are a staple food around April-May, and *mukulpa* means the carved wooden barb on the throwing-spear and the hook for the spearthrower. Sometimes, too, there are special terms for concepts which have no English equivalents, like *tjukurpa* (best translated as "dreamtime" or "dreaming"), a word denoting an idea of time and human destiny which is unique to these people and must be described in detail in order to make sense to an English-speaker.

The particularism of some of the vocabulary is offset, however, by the fluidity of meaning carried by other, important words. Many frequently used nouns convert easily into verbs by arbitrary assignment to one of four verb classes and the addition of the appropriate suffixes to indicate person, number, tense, and so forth. For example, the noun *wangka* (speech, language) also appears as the verb *wangka* (talk, speak), one of the so-called zero-class verbs which lack a suffix in the command form and the verb stem. Also, many words have a broad range of meaning which makes them readily adaptable to a variety of situations. An example is the verb *puwa* (push, pound, strike), which can be used in almost any situation where the idea of giving impetus or force is important. It means the physical act of striking, as when a man clubs an animal, but it can also mean giving strength to an argument, as when a man speaks forcefully, or to a song, by singing with vigor and emphasis. Another example is the noun *yapu* (stone, rock), which means the substance of stone or rock, regardless of dimension and shape, and can be applied to any rocky thing, from pebbles to mountains.

Like all languages, the Aboriginal language is constantly changing, particularly with regard to the vocabulary. Some of this change is due to contact with whites. Among Aborigines living on missions, reserves, and homesteads there are new words for the white man's "gadgets." One sign of the present strength of the native language is the way English words for things are reshaped in terms of the Aboriginal phonology. In Aboriginal speech, certain sounds occur which have no counterparts in English, and vice versa. I am reminded of the frustration once experienced by the headmaster of the government school at Warburton. Faced with about a dozen young Aborigines just off the desert, he began their first English lesson with a standard elementary primer which starts with the sentence, "Fluff is here." This could not have been worse-chosen, for there are no *f, s,* or *h* sounds in the Ngatatjara dialect. The Aboriginal children simply did not distinguish these sounds or attach any meaning to them.

Also, certain sounds belong together, while others do not. For example, every Aboriginal word must end with a vowel, so English words being adapted for Aboriginal use must often be given a vowel suffix, simply to complete this pattern. Also, under Aboriginal rules, certain consonants can never occur together but must be divided by a vowel, so vowels must be inserted into some English words to make them conform to traditional canons of speech. The following list shows some of the effects of these adaptations:

apple	*yapulpa*
boss	*pu:rpa*
cigarette	*tjikirpa*
chisel	*tjitjilpa*
damper	*tampa*
government official	*kapamanpa* ("government man")
helicopter	*yalikapta*
motorcar	*mutuka*
pussycat	*putjika*
rabbit	*ṛapita*
silver(ware)	*pilyalpa*
sugar	*tukatji*
truck	*tuṛaka*
"whitefella"	*walypala*
white woman	*mitjitji* (from "Mrs.")
wild cat	*wi:lyka*

These are fairly simple changes, in which English words have been adopted directly and reshaped into their Aboriginal equivalents. But some of the indirect changes are even more fascinating, for instance, the Aboriginal word for "billycan." Anyone who has listened to the song "Waltzing Matilda" has heard of this Australian national institution, essential to the vital (to Australians) business of boiling tea while traveling in the bush. Usually a billycan (or "billy") is nothing more than a large tin can with a simple handle made of fencing wire. The Aboriginal word for this item is *wayatjara. Waya* = wire, and the suffix *-tjara* means "having" or "that which has." Thus analyzed, *wayatjara* means "that which has [a] wire."

Not all linguistic changes are the result of culture-contact. Even without the presence of Europeans, the Aboriginal language is constantly undergoing basic changes. The most important single mechanism for such indigenous change is the strict practice of never uttering the name of a person who has died. Since these personal names sometimes are, or sound, the same as names of basic objects such as parts of the body, this practice may cause the previous terms for these objects to drop out of use. Several years ago at Warburton Ranges a person named Ngayunya died. The stem of the first person singular pronoun is *ngayu-,* which was abandoned at that time in favor of the stem *nganku-,* a form which until then had been used in addressing one's mother-in-law. However, a few years later the death of another person with a name which sounded like *nganku-* led to the reestablishment of the stem *ngayu-* for "I." [21] By the time my wife and I arrived at the Warburton Ranges in 1966, this stem had again been fully accepted as normal usage. It was also owing to a death that the word *tjitji* (child) was replaced shortly before our arrival by *tjilku,* a change which still remained in effect when we left in June 1967. Following this rule, a new word will have to be found to replace *muṭi* (knee) when Muṭinya, an aged Ngatatjara man at Warburton, dies. For people having the same name as the deceased the usual practice is to abandon the name in favor of the general appellation *kunmanara,* or else to adopt a new name. This rule applies to "whitefella" names, too, and during our stay at Warburton Ranges all the Normans changed to Wally for this reason. Also, owing to an earlier death, the name Philip could not be uttered. Needless to say this practice makes things difficult for census-takers and other government officials and can sometimes make it hard for the anthropologist to collect genealogies.

Many Aborigines also are familiar enough with neighboring dialects to be able to "switch" and converse in a dialect other than their own. This sometimes occurs as a mark of courtesy when making a visit to some neighboring group. Aborigines are very "speech conscious" and are quick to notice any phrases or constructions that differ from those of their own dialects. They are keenly interested in the different dialects they hear and generally absorb the differences quickly. One young Ngatatjara man now living at Warburton married a woman from the country around Ernabella Mission, about 300 miles east. Later his father-in-law came to Warburton to live, and there both he and his father-in-law tend to use the Ngatatjara dialect. Ngatatjara speech calls for an initial consonant on all words, but the Ernabella dialect allows certain words to begin with a vowel. Words spoken as *yingka* (sing) and *yuwa* (yes) at Warburton become *ingka* and *uwa* when spoken at Ernabella. However, on long trips which I took with them in the bush, both men tended to adopt the Ernabella mode of speech, a switch which I interpret as a sign of respect and deference shown by the young man toward his father-in-law. The young man was particularly careful to do this when we traveled eastward toward the Ernabella region and along the way encountered people who were walking west from there.

The Gibson Desert Aborigines sometimes gesture as they speak, but in addition they can communicate entirely by gesturing. As is the spoken language, these signs are understood over a wide area of the desert. Among some groups of people, such as the Indians of the Great Plains of North America, sign language was important as a kind of universal medium of communication between groups speaking different languages. Sign language does not seem to be as important for the desert Aborigines, however, who use it mainly to communicate in situations that demand silence. For example, men waiting for game in a hunting blind, or stalking a kangaroo, can signal to each other noiselessly without frightening the animals away. Many of the signals indicate different game animals and elements of their behavior. Also, sign language is used at ceremonies, when initiated men wish to discuss their plans without the novices overhearing.

Although we never mastered the full repertoire, my wife and I learned a few of the more commonly used signs. Some of the hand signals are clearly visible over long distances, making it

possible for people to communicate beyond voice range or on
windy days when it is hard to hear a shouted message. Since our
return from the bush we have found some of the signs convenient
when we want to communicate with each other at parties without
attracting the attention of the host or the other guests. If, for example, I am getting sleepy and think we should go home, I might
signal:

I   sleep   (implying we should leave)

Depending on what she wants to do, she might signal back:

what?   wait

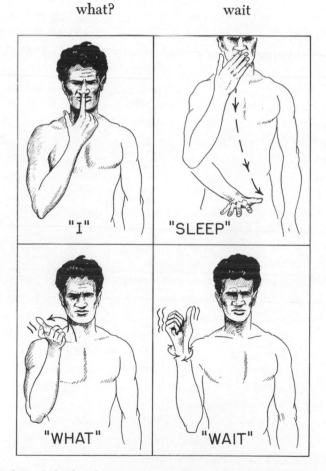

A few of the hand signs commonly used by the Aborigines.

Although this brief description cannot hope to convey the full range of subtlety and richness of the Pitjantjara language, it should indicate that the speech of the desert Aborigines is not in any way "primitive" or "simple." Moreover, the desert people have shown an ability systematically to adapt their language to the changed conditions brought on by European contact. They are an excellent example of the comment of the distinguished American linguist Edward Sapir that ". . . language is an essentially perfect means of expression and communication among every known people." [22]

The Satisfactions of Survival

There is a school of homespun philosophy which asserts that "you only get out of something what you put into it." This idea, trite as it may seem, can be applied to the daily life of the Aborigines. The varied and specialized activities of civilization are distracting, and in this age it is easy to forget that the supreme human achievement *is* survival and that all other human achievements follow from it. The desert Aborigines never forget this. The day-to-day business of survival mobilizes most of their thoughts and actions with the kind of absorption in the task that characterizes the dedicated chess player or sailboat-racing expert. For the Aborigines survival means not only keeping oneself and one's relatives alive but deriving satisfaction from having done so by one's own cleverness, skill, and physical endurance.

72

Mutual Curiosity

The experience of each anthropologist varies with the group he studies. Some find "their people" cooperative and friendly; others find theirs suspicious and hostile. But all must reach some kind of working arrangement whereby they can participate in the lives of the people they are studying without actually becoming natives themselves. That is, the anthropologist must remain an outsider, if for no other reason than to preserve his objectivity. In our case, our position as outsiders, and Americans at that, was a definite advantage at times.

Although Mitapuyi, Katapi, and the others do not speak English, in their short sojourn at the Warburton Ranges Mission (where we first knew them) they heard English spoken by the mission staff and government officers, all of whom are Australians and speak with noticeable Australian accents. As I mentioned in the preceding chapter, Aborigines are "speech conscious"; the group soon realized that my wife and I spoke a dialect of English that differed from that of the other whites. As we learned the Ngatatjara language better we realized that for some time this difference in dialect had been a cause of speculation. To them the use of a different dialect implies that the speaker comes from some place far away, and they drew the logical conclusion that we must have come from a place far from the homes of the other whites stationed at Warburton. Soon we realized that, although they were shy about asking direct questions, these people were enormously curious about us. In short, we were a novelty in their lives.

We decided to cultivate this curiosity by answering their questions and showing them pictures in magazines we sometimes received from the United States. Pictures of buildings, airplanes, automobiles, and other objects left them singularly unimpressed. They would show a polite interest and go on to something else. But pictures of people and scenery fascinated them. For instance, Nyurapaya might point to a photograph of some politicians in a copy of *Time* magazine and ask how these people were related to me. Then I would have to explain that there are far too many people in America, not to mention the rest of the world, for all of them to be related. Since the desert Aborigines do not count beyond five (after which the word *piṇi*—"many"—must suffice), it was impossible for me to convey effectively what vast numbers of people inhabit these places. But Nyurapaya and the others soon discovered that the myriads of people in the magazine pictures were all different, and this impressed them. Pictures of Negroes always aroused interest. I would be asked if these dark-skinned people were Aborigines like themselves, which would lead to an explanation about African and American Negroes. It always interested them to see a picture of a dark-skinned person driving a vehicle or operating machinery—activities which their previous experiences had led them to believe were almost always performed by whites.

Pictures of scenery and landscapes had a profound effect. The adults always wanted to know where a place shown in a picture was located and if it was anything like the place we came from. Desert scenes usually elicited comparisons with places they knew. A picture of a ship at sea aroused exclamations, not for the ship, but for the incredible amount of water in the scene. They of course have never seen the ocean or even a substantial river. Pictures of animals interested but at the same time puzzled them. A moose, an elephant, a rhinoceros, a huge Maine lobster, a fawn with its mother, fish—what kinds of animals were these? They recognized camels, cats, and rabbits at once, since these have run wild in the Australian desert ever since they were first introduced by Europeans. Cattle and horses, too, were familiar, since there are some of these at Warburton. But the other animals required explanation, and we tried our best to provide it.

Inevitably the desert people learned that in America there are no kangaroos, spinifex, emus, mulga, or Aborigines. One hot afternoon, Mitapuyi, leafing through a copy of *The New Yorker*, exclaimed, "*Lara ṇiṇu* [Wow, it's a rabbit-eared bandicoot]!" and rushed over to show me the picture. Sure enough, near the bottom of the column, apropos of nothing else on the page, was a small but unmistakable drawing of this uniquely Australian marsupial. I was as surprised as Mitapuyi to see it there, and I said so. Now and then, a kangaroo would appear in a Qantas Airways advertisement, but such appearances were relatively rare.

Although we had not really planned it, the magazines became a useful aid to our studies, for they helped evoke an atmosphere of mutual curiosity between the Aborigines and ourselves. In time the reluctance to ask us direct questions disappeared, and we often found ourselves being interviewed about our relatives, the places we had lived, and a variety of other things like writing, songs, and the trivia of our daily lives (such as brushing our teeth, an endless source of speculation). It became possible to explain that we came from America, a place which they could understand was a very long way off, where the people were generally ignorant about the Aborigines and wanted to know how they lived. We explained that this was our reason for living with them and that we needed their help.

The paramount question in their minds all along had been: why were my wife and I living in the desert with the Aborigines? For a time there had been a lingering suspicion or fear of unknown motives which made progress in our studies slow and to some extent superficial. Their realization that our curiosity and that of other people in America was not unlike their own curiosity about us made a big difference. It brought to the surface a basic pride which the desert Aborigines have in their accomplishment of living in what they acknowledge is a harsh environment. They recognized that we were seriously interested in knowing the minute details of their daily existence in order to understand this accomplishment. Their response was to take our "education" quite seriously and they began going out of their way to point out different species of edible plants and animals and explaining or showing how these are gathered and prepared. This attitude also led them to show us the broad range of their technology and economy, including behavior having to do with their sacred life. On a couple of occasions I was even reprimanded for apparent inattention to something they were showing or telling me, because I was not immediately writing it all down in my notebook. They saw their role as that of teachers, and they never hesitated to rouse me if something new or interesting occurred. Indeed, in some respects, this became anthropology made easy. From their behavior toward us I came to

see that the use of their wide knowledge of the particular resources of the desert led not only to their physical survival but to
a deep feeling of accomplishment and intellectual pleasure which
was its own reward. At this stage my anthropological fieldwork
began to go beyond the original scholarly objectives and became
a personally enjoyable experience. I had a firsthand realization,
quite apart from any romanticizing or wishful thinking on my
part, that the desert Aborigines led lives which were rewarding
and satisfying to them.

Traveling Light

Because they must always be able to move from one waterhole to the next, every item of the material culture of the desert
Aborigines must be completely portable. Most of the tools used
by the Ngatatjara are extremely light and easy to carry. Spears,
clubs, wooden bowls, and digging-sticks are both indispensable
and light. These people do not use boomerangs, but they are
aware of them, as the Australian anthropologist Norman B. Tindale discovered in 1935 when he collected from Aborigines living
near the Warburton Ranges a series of myths which includes an
account of boomerangs and how they are used.[1] The Ngatatjara
even have a word for the returning boomerang (*kaḷi*), but for
reasons which remain mysterious they do not use the weapon.
However, some of the Gibson Desert Aborigines have a thin,
curved wooden throwing-stick which they call *walanu.* This is
thrown overhand at small game and flies straight, without returning. Often these throwing-sticks are decorated by carving a
series of fine parallel lines on one side.

In order to leave the hands free while foraging, items like
clubs and throwing-sticks are tucked into a string belt or girdle.
These belts are fashioned from human hair and coated with red
ocher and emu fat to keep them from getting brittle in the dry
desert heat. Lizards, rabbits, and other small game picked up
during the day are also tucked into the belt. I once saw a man
at the end of the day with a large catch of rabbits and a feral
cat. The profusion of fluffy bodies tucked into his string belt was
so great he had the appearance of wearing a skirt.

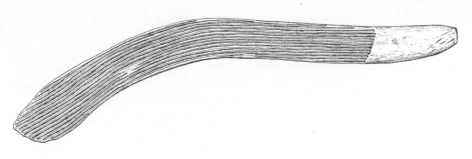

A throwing-stick (*walanu*) from the Gibson Desert.

Hand-held grinding stones are fairly easy for the women to carry from place to place, but the heavy grinding-slabs of rock constitute a problem. These are generally carried from the quarry where they are found to campsites where they will be used and left permanently. Campsites with stone grinding-slabs are strategically situated as near as possible to places where wild seeds or other plant resources that require grinding occur. Whenever such grinding-slabs are encountered at a campsite, it is an elementary rule of desert courtesy to leave them in place. Often they have been carried a long way by the owner, as were, for example, the grinding-slabs at Tika-tika, a campsite about forty miles from Partjar. Some of these stone slabs may weigh as much as thirty pounds, and Aborigine women are understandably annoyed when they discover that some "whitefella" passing through the bush (perhaps on a mineral or topographic survey) has carried theirs away as a souvenir.

The portability of certain tools is enhanced by their multifunctional character. The ultimate example of a multipurpose tool in the Gibson Desert is the spearthrower, called *miru* or *langkuru*. Spearthrowers are known to be ancient hunting weapons in several parts of the world. On the basis of archaeological evidence they are thought to have been present in the Upper Paleolithic cultures of Europe and among the Paleo-Indians of the New World. More recently, they were used by the Arctic Eskimo and several American Indian groups, including the Aztec, who called the weapon the *atlatl*. The desert Aborigines of Australia are the last people in the world to make extensive use of this ancient type of weapon. In many parts of the world the spearthrower was supplanted by the bow and arrow, but, except possibly among some people living along the northern coast of Queensland, this did not happen in Australia.

The Australian desert spearthrower is an elliptical-shaped wooden instrument, usually about thirty inches long and about four inches wide, with a knob of spinifex resin at one end for the handle and a small hardwood hook or spur fastened on at the other end with sinew. The broad blade of the weapon's shaft is often carved to a deeply concave shape, and among the desert people it is not unusual to find spearthrower blades decorated with complex incised designs. Usually there is a flake of chipped quartzite or chert set into the resin handle. The whole instrument rarely weighs over a pound.

The langkuru acts as a throwing board to give extra leverage to the cast of the spear. Tongue in cheek, American anthropologist and writer Harold S. Gladwin tells how to use an Australian spearthrower:

"Now fit your fingers into the notches [on either side of the handle] and grip the spearthrower with the spur on the top side. Engage the cupped end of a dart with the spur so that the dart lies flat along the handle between your first and second fingers, or, if this feels clumsy, steady the dart with your left hand. When you have followed all of these instructions and are ready to test your skill, make your cast with an overarm motion, just as throwing a stone. Then, if all goes well, you may be able to hit the broad side of a barn at thirty paces." [2]

It takes long practice to acquire skill with this weapon. One can hurl a spear as far as 100 yards using a spearthrower, but real accuracy is possible only up to about 120 feet. By this I mean that an Aborigine man who uses a spearthrower regularly can consistently hit a 2-by-2-foot target at this distance, usually by direct flight with the spear but also, at times, by bouncing or skimming the spear off the ground so it rises into the target. Either way, the spear strikes with considerable force. With practice in using a spearthrower I developed the ability to throw a spear for distances of up to 200 and 300 feet, but even at close range my accuracy always left something to be desired. Often the hook would slip out of the hole in the end of the spear just as I was about to throw, and as my arm snapped forward the spear would flop ignominiously to the ground. This amused my mentors, who patiently picked up the spear and encouraged me to try again. For my frustrations, however, I was rewarded with the realization that there is considerable individual variation in technique when using this weapon. The grip on the handle is fairly uniform for everyone, but the left hand may grip the spearshaft, prop it up, or leave it alone, according to the preference of the individual. Some men lean back as they get ready to throw, raising their front foot which they swing forward and bring down during the cast to give extra force, while others prefer a slightly crouching stance with the throwing arm doing most of the work.

This instrument is best known for its role in throwing spears, but it has several other important functions as well. These include use as a friction-stick in firemaking, as a tray for mixing pigments and for mixing tobacco with ash, as a percussion instrument which is tapped for rhythm at certain ceremonies, as a kind of scraping shovel for clearing thorns and pebbles from a patch of ground where people plan to sit or camp, and as a woodworking tool, by means of the stone flake attached to the handle. This last use is highly characteristic of the desert Aborigines. The work is done in a seated position, with the operator cradling in his lap the piece of wood to be shaped, while he grips the spear-thrower handle in one hand, drawing it smoothly and firmly toward his body along the surface of the wooden object. By repeating this process, he scrapes the shavings away until the wooden item acquires the desired shape. From time to time he has to interrupt the work to resharpen the stone flake, either by biting away the chips (most often with the premolar teeth, but sometimes with molars or canines, according to personal preference) or by gently tapping them off with a piece of wood used as a striker. In general these hafted stone flakes (called adzes by many Australian archaeologists) are surprisingly efficient, and to shape a wooden artifact this way normally takes only about twice as long as it does with metal tools.

One day as I sat in camp near the Warburton Mission talking with Mitapuyi's younger brother, Tjun, I witnessed what may be the absolute epitome of this principle of portability in Aboriginal life. Tjun was putting the finishing touches on a spearthrower he had been making, on and off, over the previous two weeks. It looked complete except for the all-important hook. I asked him, "*Mukulpa wanytjatja* [Where is the hook]?" Instead of replying, he reached up inside his nose and extracted a double-pointed piece of mulga wood about an inch long, which he fastened to the end of the spearthrower with some sinew. As he explained later, a hole is punched in the septum of the nose as one of a series of physical ordeals that men progress through in their sacred life, and this hole has to be kept open or in time it will heal shut. Tjun rarely wore a bone noseplug, but he liked to keep an extra double-pointed piece of wood in the hole as a spare spearthrower hook or spear-barb. His nose, like that of most Aborigines, was extremely broad and completely covered the wooden piece when it was inserted, so a casual visitor might easily fail to observe it. Upon inquiring later I found that many of the desert Aborigines engaged in this practice. By carrying the piece of wood in the nose the hands are left free, yet the wood is instantly available to replace a worn hook or barb during a hunt or while traveling. Not only does it keep the nose hole from healing shut, but, there is no danger of forgetting where one has left this useful object in time of need.

Dr. Donald F. Thomson, Professor of Anthropology at the University of Melbourne, has suggested another use for spear-throwers of the decorated variety. He stated that the decoration shown to him ". . . was really a map, highly conventionalized, like the marks on a 'message' or 'letter' stick of the aborigines, of the waters of the vast terrain over which [the aborigines] hunted." [3] For the Gibson Desert people this is true, but only indirectly. On spearthrowers, as on sacred boards, a variety of incised designs may be used, generally to represent the same basic theme: a series of named water sources along the track of a mythical totemic ancestor. Sometimes other landmarks, such as sandhills, rocky outcrops, or salt lakes, are also shown. Not all the water sources of a region are included in the series, but only those thought to have been visited or created in the dreamtime by the particular mythological character being represented. The designs on spearthrowers, as on sacred boards, serve as mnemonic devices for recalling the sacred tradition in its correct sequence by calling to mind the particular songs which evoke the mythological events occurring at each place. Incidental designs related to the central theme also occur: long connecting lines (a representation of the ancestor's track) or parallel zigzag lines with diagonal hatching (the women's dance ground at a particular sacred site). Unlike sacred boards, decorated spearthrowers are not kept hidden but are carried about in camp and on the move where all can see them, but the sacred stories and place-names represented by the designs are never revealed to women or uninitiated men. I have no evidence to show that decorated spearthrowers are consulted as maps in the strictly practical sense (as Thomson suggests). Rather, as mnemonic devices for recalling sacred traditions on ritual occasions, they indirectly reinforce and pass on vital knowledge about local desert terrain.

As a multipurpose tool the desert spearthrower always reminded me of a jackknife I owned as a youngster. This had several blades and could serve as a screwdriver, corkscrew, nailfile, awl, and bottle and can opener, in addition to being a knife. All of this was compact and easy to carry. Indeed, I sometimes wonder why the tool was even called a knife, since it could be used for so many things in addition to cutting. Now I wonder the same thing about the English word for the spearthrower. The native terms for this object do not emphasize one particular function over the others; instead, they denote the distinctive form of the object and imply all of its many functions as well. This concept becomes clearer when one sees how tools like the spearthrower are made.

Ideas, in fact, are the most portable and useful tools there are. The Aboriginal tool kit is not impressive to look at, but traveling with Aborigines deep in the desert and seeing them cope from day to day with the problems of survival makes one appreciate their knowledge both of local resources and of techniques. Much of the Aboriginal tool kit is ephemeral and easily overlooked by the casual observer.

My first reaction to Aboriginal tools was much the same as that of many other observers before me. Their apparent crudeness and simplicity, and the small number of types, caused initial disappointment. Indeed, there was not much to see: a few stone chips, a handful (literally) of wooden tools, and a few items made from human hair-string. Compared to the intricate and ingenious devices of some other hunting-and-gathering societies, such as the Eskimo, this seemed a pretty poor showing. But longer association with Aborigines in the bush changed my opinion completely. As is so often true of these desert dwellers, apparent simplicity only masked the true complexities of their behavior.

For example, consider what I shall call "instant tools." One morning I watched Nyurapaya as she prepared to go out to collect wild seeds. Before picking up her wooden bowl she wandered around the camp for a few minutes, in what seemed to be an aimless manner. She explained that she needed a *manguṛi,* the circular pad used to balance and cushion the load on her head. I thought she meant that she had misplaced a ready-made hair-string manguṛi, and I started looking for it myself. At this point she laughed and pointed to a tuft of long, greenish grass, saying "*Nga:tja manguṛi pinpa* [Here is one like a load-cushioning pad]." I was puzzled but before I had time to ask any questions she seized the bunch of grass and twisted and knotted it into a simple circlet which she placed on her head. Later I learned that she had given her hair-string pad to a relative. After the day's foraging, Nyurapaya tossed the grass circlet off into the bush, since she could make another just like it the next day.

On another occasion my wife went foraging with some Ngatatjara women near Laverton. The Aborigines at this place live close to a small town and have much more regular contact with whites than the Aborigines at Warburton Mission do. One of the women had with her a large dog, evidently a cross between a dingo and a sheep rancher's dog. Unlike the true desert Aborigines, she had trained this dog to chase and kill kangaroos, and later in the day it did kill one. My wife watched as one of the women picked up a sharp flake of natural quartzite and, holding it between thumb and forefinger, used it to make an incision in the kangaroo's belly to remove the intestines. When she had finished, she tossed the stone off to one side and it was left behind—until my wife came back and got it for the collection of Aboriginal artifacts we were making.

Sitting in camp, I sometimes saw men sharpening spear tips or scraping a few shavings from a spear shaft or digging-stick with a plain, untrimmed flake of chert or quartzite. This happened when, for one reason or another, the men did not have their spearthrowers (with stone adzes attached to the handles). On the Native Reserves close to the Warburton Mission and the town of Laverton I saw men use fragments of glass from broken bottles in the same way. After the task at hand was completed, the flakes were simply tossed aside and abandoned.

I have already described the use of naturally smooth stones to pound together and shred the meat, skin, and bones of certain goannas. Plain, untrimmed stones are also used to pound wooden wedges used in butchering kangaroos and emus and in removing slabs from tree trunks for making spearthrowers. A large stone with a naturally sharp edge may be used as a simple handax for heavy woodworking tasks. At the completion of the task these stones are abandoned where they were used.

In each of these cases (and there are many others like them) the tool needed for a particular task was obtained from some natural object or material immediately at hand and after being used was discarded. It had no value except as a means of solving an immediate practical problem. In most cases there was no attempt to modify the natural material by trimming or shaping, although some of the hand-held stone scrapers acquired a distinctively concave edge through wear. Just by looking at most of these stones afterward it would be hard to tell that they had once been tools. Of course the grass circlet required some advance preparation, but this was minimal. Instant tools like these are an important part of Aboriginal culture and represent an ability to recognize potentially useful objects in the natural environment and to use them in an appropriate and efficient way. It is far more practical for the Aborigines to carry this kind of knowledge than to burden themselves with carrying the actual tools.

One day Mitapuyi mentioned in camp that he needed a new

spearthrower. His old one was split in a couple of places, and his efforts to mend the cracks with sinew had been only partly successful. At the time there seemed to be little response to his comment, but the next day Katapi said to him, "*Ngayulu langkuru nyangu* [I saw a spearthrower]." I thought at first that she meant she had found a ready-made spearthrower in the bush somewhere, but that did not seem to make sense. She went on to tell Mitapuyi where she had been looking for seeds that day, giving him clues so he could find the spearthrower himself when he wanted to. I was still puzzled about this when I went out with Mitapuyi a few days later to get the new spearthrower.

We walked for several hours in a leisurely way, catching a couple of lizards and finding some ngaru fruit to eat along the way. We crossed a sandhill and moved for a while along a flat, spinifex-covered area, passing through some isolated groves of mulga trees. As we approached one small patch of mulga trees Mitapuyi, pointing toward it, exclaimed, "*Lara langkuru walykumunu nyaratja* [Wow, there's a fine spearthrower over there]!" From the way he spoke, I still half-expected to see a ready-made spearthrower leaning up against a tree or bush. But as we reached the grove he indicated a large mulga tree with a trunk straighter than most. He and Katapi had meant that in this grove there was a tree with wood of shape and quality suitable for making a spearthrower. They shared an understanding of what sort of tree would yield an acceptable spearthrower, and their conversation was based on this fact. The other trees we had seen on our way were not deemed suitable for this purpose; hence they were ignored.

In thinking about this experience I was reminded of the concept proposed by Dr. James Deetz, an American archaeologist at Brown University: "The idea of the proper form of an object exists in the mind of the maker, and when this idea is expressed in tangible form in raw material, an artifact results." [4] Deetz has aptly termed such ideas "mental templates," and the behavior I had just witnessed epitomized his proposition. Mitapuyi and Katapi had both spoken of the mulga tree as if it were in fact the spearthrower itself in its finished form. In a sense they "saw" the completed spearthrower in the shape of the tree itself and could discuss it in these terms. Subsequently, I saw this kind of behavior repeated many times for all kinds of objects, from throwing-sticks to sacred boards.

Using a steel hatchet I had given to him and a couple of wooden wedges that he fashioned on the spot, Mitapuyi removed from the mulga tree an elongated and roughly oval-shaped wooden blank for his spearthrower. He placed this on his head, and we started back for camp. Along the way he pointed out other trees which had branches or trunks shaped to yield clubs or throwing-sticks. For my benefit, he was saying aloud what he normally thought as he walked through the desert, observing and making mental notes of trees which would provide the appropriate artifacts when he might have need of them.

The silent appraisal of local resources goes on continuously as the desert people move through the bush. Details are remembered and mentioned when the family needs to know where to find raw material for this or that kind of object. In general there is little conversation while artifacts, whether of wood, stone, or fiber, are being made. Often the children look on and later try to imitate their parents' techniques with scraps of material they find lying about the camp. There is no formal instruction in these techniques aside from an occasional admonishment or correction. Most discussion, when it occurs, centers on finding the appropriate raw material. The conversations of Aborigine women arguing over where to find the right kind of spinifex-resin, or men trying to decide on the best place to look for spearwood, can become heated and vociferous. These debates, based on the recognition and recall of local resources, are vital to the maintenance of the group, since they form the basis for making decisions about when and where to move in the never-ending search for food, water, and raw materials.

I had been aware for some time that this kind of detailed knowledge about the natural environment existed among these people, but it was not until I went out from Mulyangiri, a camp near the Warburton Mission, with Mitapuyi and his maternal uncle, Minmara, to look for spearwood that I was able to appreciate firsthand the full extent and depth of this knowledge. Several kinds of plants are used in making spearshafts, the most

highly prized being the stem of a rather rare tree called *mulaṭi*.
No suitable mulaṭi wood had been seen recently in the Clutterbuck Hills or in the Warburton Ranges area, so the men decided
to look instead for *tjawu*, a species of Acacia as yet unidentified,
which has long straight roots. As might be imagined, it is no
easy matter to find a suitable piece of straight wood for an 8-
or 9-foot spearshaft in desert country where vegetation is
characteristically low and stunted. After his bad luck with the
emu at Partjaṟ, Mitapuyi had decided he wanted nothing more
to do with brittle mulga-wood spears. After considering the alternatives which he knew the local area had to offer, he settled
on tjawu roots as the best available raw material for strong and
supple spears.

The three of us set out for sandhill country where the two
men said they knew a place where good tjawu was to be found.
Eventually our trek carried us to a small isolated clump of these
low trees. Mitapuyi and Minmara walked around the grove, explaining to me that they were examining the bark on the trees.
Old trees have dry, scaly bark, while the bark of young, green
trees is smooth with a silver-gray color. In a few moments they
found a couple of young trees which they said were good. Mitapuyi walked slowly around each of these two trees, snapping
off the tips of the branches. He continued until he found some
twigs on one side of one of the trees that did not snap off easily
but merely bent without breaking. This, they agreed, was the
moist side, on which a suitable root would be found. Both men
then got down on their knees and closely examined the ground.
They were looking for minute hairline cracks in the surface
caused by pressure from a root underneath. When they found
such clues, each man fashioned an impromptu digging-stick and
dug into the soil. Within a few seconds each of them unerringly
located a thick root about ten inches below the surface. These
were exposed for their full length by digging. Neither root was
perfectly straight, but the men said that this could be remedied.

The roots were dug out of the ground, and the men immediately went to work to prepare them. Each man pulled off the
thin outer bark with his teeth and then shaved away some of
the outer wood with his hafted stone adze. The roots were al-

most exactly the right diameter, with only a few thick spots to be trimmed with the adzes. Then, Minmara used his firestick to start a small fire, and the two men waited in the shade while the fire burned down to coals. With the coals ready, Minmara placed the bent portion of his spearshaft in them and waited about twenty seconds. Then he lifted the spearshaft from the coals and holding it in both hands with the hands about two feet apart, pressed with one foot on the section between his hands to straighten it. By repeating this process for each part with a kink in it he soon·had the whole shaft straight. Minmara was especially good at this and Mitapuyi let him straighten the other spear as well. Except for the finishing touches, the spears were now completed. Aside from the decision on where to dig, the whole process was carried on in almost complete silence.

I was impressed by the way each man knew exactly what to do and did it. In the process they had taught me the technique in much the way they might teach a young son, by bringing him along with them and letting him watch. I imitated and practiced each step, while they watched, commenting briefly only when I made a mistake. I later repeated this experience many times with other objects and materials, though I by no means exhausted the full range of Aboriginal know-how of desert resources. From my sampling of this knowledge, however, I realized how hopeless it would be for any European or American to try to master this harsh environment unassisted. In addition to knowing how to prepare wild foods and raw materials, the Aborigines must know where to find the resources they want when they want them. In terms of day-to-day living, their lives from childhood on are mosaics pieced together from particular bits of experience, both firsthand and acquired through conversations with others, about where to find water, food, and the other necessities of life. These experiences are filed in their minds and recalled in times of need. For the desert people learning is a lifelong enterprise, and people are respected for their stores of knowledge. Their personal pride in their knowledge is evident whenever they make use of it, particularly in front of interested visitors like myself and my wife. What seemed to us at first to be a slow and rather monotonous way of life we now realized to be alive with intense activity and planning. The desert Aborigine walking in leisurely fashion through the bush looks as if he is doing very little. But watch his eyes. They move constantly, searching out subtle clues which his intelligence and experience help him interpret to the advantage of himself and his family, and his joy is complete and self-sufficient when he succeeds in using any of these clues to gain a valuable prize like a goanna or a fine new spear.

Familiar Tracks

When it comes to recognizing subtle clues in their environment, nothing is more impressive than the Aborigines' ability to see and "read" tracks. To many white Australians this seems an almost superhuman ability, and it is routine procedure for the police to hire Aborigines as trackers when searching for someone in the bush. Anyone who has read the exploits of Napoleon Bonaparte, the fictional half-Aborigine detective in the mystery stories by the Australian writer Arthur Upfield, has seen examples of the way white Australians sometimes attribute this ability to a kind of mystical "sixth sense."

Yet there is really no mystery about it at all. From earliest childhood, Aborigines are encouraged to examine the surface of the ground. Youngsters learn not only to identify different species of animals but to distinguish their gaits as well, and sometimes they are even able to recognize individual animals from peculiarities in their tracks. To some of the Aborigines at Laverton, seeing the tracks of a one-legged crow that has long frequented the area is like seeing an old friend—recognition is immediate. The same applies to tracks left by people. To the Aborigine a person's footprints are almost as distinctive as his physical appearance, his way of walking, or the sound of his voice. In a society where nearly all contacts between people are face to face, each individual has a lifelong opportunity to observe the tracks of those around him. It is not unusual to see an Aborigine point to some tracks out in the bush, perhaps many miles from the nearest camp or settlement, and announce the name of the person who made them. He is helped in this, of course, by his constant awareness of where the various people he knows are likely to be at a given time.

Other details such as the depth of the footprints and their relative position give further clues concerning the behavior of the person who made them. For example, deep, well-rounded heelprints indicate a healthy person with a vigorous stride. Furthermore, to the trained eye, a close examination of the edges of each print can reveal approximately how long it was since the print was made. An experienced tracker always considers the kind of soil in which the track occurs and the local weather conditions that have affected it since it was made. All these minutiae are fitted together to tell a story: "Old so-and-so, a Puṟungu man, passed this way a few days ago. He is headed for Taltiwara waterhole and is feeling all right and getting plenty to eat."

Aborigines at Work

As in all human societies, the Aborigines carry on a wide variety of activities over and above the immediate tasks of making a living. In the first chapter I showed that during a normal day plenty of spare time exists for things besides the quest for food and water. Sexual rivalries, sorcery, conflict, ritual—these were a few of the activities I mentioned in passing. But my emphasis so far has been on work, the routine trivia of making a living in the Gibson Desert.

The nature of work among the Aborigines differs greatly from that of work in civilized societies. To begin with, there is no distinction made between work and play. The two go on together, as in the case of the children at Partjaṟ collecting ngaṟu for their mothers. Individuals display special skill in certain activities, but there are no specialized occupations. Even a sorcerer with a wide reputation, like Mitapuyi, must forage for food, water, and raw materials like everyone else. Because everyone is engaged in roughly the same range of economic activities, skill in these activities and willingness to share the fruits of this skill with kin determine social prestige. In daily life there are no official leaders or privileged groups, hereditary or elected, among the Aborigines. The emphasis instead is on equality and sharing. The practical need for autonomous family groups that can forage independently in dry seasons and the nomadic movement that prevents people from accumulating possessions or large reserves of food foster these sentiments, which are inculcated through permissive child-rearing. As a result children as well as adults resent attempts at authority or pressure, particularly from their peers. It sounds like a kind of ideal communism in which everybody works and everybody shares. But it is a communism that would be difficult to apply to civilized societies. The desert Aborigines have a minimum of material possessions and are a small population living in direct personal contact, in which everyone can be classed as a relative of one sort or another of everyone else. However, in the context of the desert environment, the daily lives of the nomadic Aborigines are essentially harmonious and rewarding. An individual grows up realizing what is expected of him. By acquiring and developing practical knowledge and skill he learns to fulfill these expectations and is rewarded immediately by his own satisfaction in achievement and in the long run by the esteem of his kin. There is no room for self-deception or pomposity. Every person knows his own worth.

Gill's Pinnacle, an important sacred site, rises dramatically at the eastern end of the Rawlinson Range. The trees in the foreground are ghost gums.

Katapi and Nyurapaya forage through mulga country collecting wanguṇu seeds. The seeds are shaken into a wooden bowl and winnowed in a light breeze; after further sifting in a wooden dish, they are poured onto a flat stone and ground into flour. The seed-flour is later mixed with water and baked.

This Ngatatjara man, throwing a spear by means of a spearthrower, stands with his back straight and his left hand free. Minmara (below) uses a different style, resting the spearshaft on his left wrist and leaning back before starting his throw. Both photographs were taken at the precise moment when the man was about to throw the spear forward.

A characteristic way to hold a spear when using a spearthrower.

Today long stretches of the Woomera Rocket Range access road—the "Gunbarrel Highway"—have been washed into this condition.

Kunmanara pounds a wooden wedge into the side of a mulga tree to separate a slab of wood intended for a spearthrower. The designs on his body were painted for a ceremony in which he took part earlier that day. After the preliminary work with wedges, he pries the slab loose from the tree. In this instance the initial cut was made with a steel ax, but stone handaxes are still used now and then.

Minmara chips a stone tool with his teeth. The Gibson Desert Aborigines are the only people known to use this technique today. Other stone-chipping techniques practiced in the area include gentle percussion-flaking by means of a wooden baton or striker, and direct percussion with a hammerstone.

The long roots of the tjawu or ironwood tree are prized for making tough supple spearshafts. After careful examination Mitapuyi digs out a root. Using his teeth, he strips the thin outer bark from the root; then with a stone adze-flake hafted to the end of his spearthrower he trims the root to an even diameter. Minmara, adept at the task, does the final straightening, first heating the shaft in the coals of a small fire, and then bending it straight.

Mitapuyi grins with pleasure on catching a small goanna. His missing front tooth was knocked out in one of a series of ordeals during his initiation into the sacred life.

Two elderly Ngatatjara men with bodies painted for a Tingari-cycle ceremony.

5

Desert Rituals and the Sacred Life

During the hottest part of the year, around February-March, great cyclonic storms move erratically over the Gibson Desert. In the late afternoon the clouds gather in lines, looking like the sails of an immense armada cruising out across the sandhills. These storms, stately and calm when viewed at a distance, send out violent bursts of hot wind as they get closer. In most instances these summer storms are all bluster and hot air, with little else to mark their passage. But at times they develop into drenching squalls, pouring out as much as the yearly average of rainfall in the space of a few hours. At night such storms produce almost continuous lightning, with hail, wind, and curtains of torrential rain combining to create a cacophonous spectacle which the Aborigines dread. No shelter of theirs can protect them from this kind of storm. The shade-shelters in which they huddle shield them about as well as would a wicker basket under a waterfall. Soaked to the skin, they sit together, trying to keep warm with lighted firesticks held close to their bodies.

Nothing looks more abject than an Aborigine camp after one of these storms. The dogs are the saddest sight. They are scrawny to begin with, and the deluge leaves their hair matted close to their bodies, so their ribs stick out and they look even more emaciated than usual. The people usually sit quietly, suffering the chill of the wind on their wet bodies in silence. Sometimes a fire is built up (mulga wood burns well even when wet), and the people stand close to it to get dry. Spears and spearthrowers lie in the mud where the storm has blown them. Worst of all, caches of food are blown down from the trees in which they were stored. The dogs are usually quick to rush in and make away with whatever food they can seize. Men, women, and children all grab burning fagots to throw at the dogs, shouting or hissing *"Payi"* with as much menace as they can put into their voices, but this rarely does much good, and the dogs have an uncommonly fine feast.

Although they detest the wet and the cold, the Aborigines realize how vital these rains are to their well-being. Their spirits rise as the sun appears and the day grows warmer and there is time to think beyond immediate discomforts to the effects of the rains on their daily routine. Lacking any clearly defined system of drainage to follow, the rainwater usually ends up as broad but shallow pools filling low spots between the sandhills. With repeated rains these pools may grow to large sheets of fresh water several miles long, with broad borders of liquid mud. Among white Australians who travel through the bush it is a rule of thumb to allow a week of drying for every inch of rain before attempting to drive through these wet spots. But the Aborigines have no vehicles or pack animals to worry about, and they take advantage of the abundance of water and of game that follows these heavy local rains to hunt and forage in country far removed from their more permanent waters. This situation also gives families a chance to come together for a time, while supplies of food and water are abundant enough in one area to sustain a large group. Norman Tindale has reported gatherings of as many as 270 individuals among the Pitjantjara-speaking Aborigines in country about 300 miles east of the Warburton Ranges,[1] but in the Gibson Desert gatherings of more than 150 were probably uncommon.

Large gatherings like these generate excitement. There are opportunities for gossip and sexual adventures (discreetly pursued but very intense). Long-separated relatives are reunited, and marriage prospects are investigated. Domestic arguments break out, too, as jealousies flare. Many desert Aborigines are polygynous—that is, the men have two or more wives—and a husband sometimes finds it difficult at times like these to keep an eye on all his wives. But above all there are opportunities for ritual and ceremony.

The daily life of the Aborigines is rewarding but routine. There is a kind of low-key pace to the everyday round of living. In their ritual lives, however, the Aborigines attain a heightened sense of drama. Sharp images appear and colors deepen. The Aborigines are masters of stagecraft and achieve remarkable visual and musical effects with the limited materials at hand. Although some of the ritual practices seem at first glance to be bizarre and even sadistic, their ceremonial life is notable for meditation and sobriety rather than for frenzy.

There are several excellent scholarly accounts of Aboriginal religious and ritual practices as well as detailed descriptions of traditional beliefs and ceremonial organization.[2] Reading these in preparation for going into the field, made me aware of the complexities of Aboriginal religion, but my understanding of the sacred life still seemed incomplete. I could not share in the emotional satisfaction brought about by these beliefs and practices. They seemed too much like intellectual exercises which left me impressed but unmoved. Instead of being exhilarated after I witnessed my first ceremonies, I felt depressed and inadequate to the task of understanding. What was wrong?

At first I blamed the Aborigines. These short dances and songs seemed like mere powderpuffs. How could anyone take such spiritual tidbits seriously? Since I knew that a complicated social organization and theology underlie the rituals, I was taken aback by the seeming insignificance of the pantomimes.

The fault was with my own understanding. Not until I saw the Aborigines in the desert, living under nomadic conditions in the regions they normally frequented, did I realize how deeply I had misjudged their religion. In time I watched many more ceremonies and participated in a few, and my understanding of and delight in them grew. Gradually I experienced the central truth of Aboriginal religion: that it is not a thing by itself but an inseparable part of a whole that encompasses every aspect of daily life, every individual, and every time—past, present, and future. It is nothing less than the theme of existence, and as such constitutes one of the most sophisticated and unique religious and philosophical systems known to man. Professor Emile Durkheim, a distinguished French sociologist, writing about forty years ago, contrasted the sacred and profane aspects of Aboriginal life.[3] If not interpreted too literally, this is a useful distinction for describing Aboriginal ceremonies, since separation of the sexes during important ceremonies and separation of daily activities from ritual actors and events function to varying degrees in most ceremonial activities. But I found Durkheim's framework more of a hindrance than a help in appreciating the Aboriginal religion. For me the striking thing was the absolute relevance of every part of it to the problems and situations of daily life. In a sense, everything within the Aborigines' environment is holy, not in some vague, pantheistic sense but in terms of concrete ties which the rituals use and revitalize.

Rather than attempt a formal description of Aboriginal religion, I prefer to describe certain rituals which I witnessed and which were illuminating and significant to me. Each is quite different from the others and each reveals a wide area of Aboriginal belief. There is much more to Aboriginal religion than these particular rituals, but since they epitomize the essential elements better than most they will serve as a guide to the general character of Aboriginal beliefs and ceremonies.

Marks of Manhood

The shouting had barely begun when a woman ran up to me saying, "*Maḷulu pitjangu* [The kangaroo-novice came]." I went out in time to see a young man with a string cord tied around his head walking out to the creekbed with a group of older men. This lad had left Warburton about a year ago with his maternal uncle and has now returned along with a group of men from the reserves at Ernabella and Musgrave Park in South Australia. In addition to these places he had also visited the reserve at Areyonga in Northern Territory. Now he is going out to the secluded camp where two other novices are living.

The three novices, all between about thirteen and sixteen years of age, know they will be circumcised soon, but exactly when and how they are not sure. They live together in a camp in the bush while their relatives in the main camp send food out to them. The one already mentioned has had the good fortune to make the "grand tour" with his mother's brother, visiting distant camps where he was shown sacred dances and taught sacred songs. The other two have been at the bush camp for about three months; their range of sacred knowledge when they are circumcised will be far less than his. However, since a large group of Warburton and Musgrave Park people is now gathered together, the prevailing sentiment is that all three boys should be operated on at the same time.

The novices have mixed feelings. They can imagine the pain only too well and are nervous and apprehensive. But they also know the whole community will be watching them and that their present behavior will be discussed for the rest of their lives. They are proud to have this opportunity to make a public show of their physical courage.

During their seclusion they are introduced to sacred dances and songs to an extent that they have never experienced before. The actual ordeal comes as the climax following a buildup lasting as long as five or six weeks. The songs and dances which the boys are taught are short and episodic. In highly abbreviated form they re-enact adventures and events in the lives of mythological beings that lived in the "dreamtime" (*tjukurpa*). The Pitjantjara word indicates a kind of timeless mythical past during which totemic beings traveled from place to place across the desert performing creative acts. Some of these beings are natural species of the region, such as the opossum, kangaroo, echidna (spiny anteater), dingo, marsupial cat, bush turkey, emu, eagle, rabbit-eared bandicoot, bat, carpet snake, "mountain devil" lizard, magpie, and goanna, but there are other special ones, among them Wati Kutjara (the Two Men), Waṇampi (the Water-snake), and Yula (Penis). The "tracks" or routes taken by these beings in the dreamtime lace the desert in all directions, often crossing and recrossing.[4] Although they lived in the past, the dreamtime beings are still thought of as being alive and exerting influence over present-day people. While the dancers prepare, the novices lie on the ground, face down, with eyes closed. When each dance begins they sit up but may not look directly at the performance. One lad holds his hand in front of his face and peers out between his fingers, while the others avert their eyes slightly to one side. They have not yet reached the level of sacred knowledge at which they can look directly at the dances without fear of illness.

Singing usually begins in the early afternoon and may continue until the next morning, then be resumed the next afternoon, and so on. The men sit in two circles, representing a division which runs through the entire society. One circle calls itself "sun," the other "shade." Each circle consists of men who belong to generations which alternate with those of the opposite circle. For example, I sit on the sun side with men of my own generation as well as those of my grandfather's and my grandson's generations (these generations are called *nganatarka*). Opposite me, in the shade circle, sit men of my father's and my son's generations (called *tarpuṭa*). The men in each circle sit facing inward, and each man grasps a stick in front of him. During songs, rhythm is maintained by pounding the sticks on the ground. This rhythmic pounding is said to be the sound of the mythological kangaroos' tails thumping against the ground as they hopped from one place to the next in the dreamtime. After a while this pounding creates a depression in the soil underneath the stick, and each song-circle has a ring of these depressions radiating out like spokes on a wheel. These are said to be the sleeping grounds of the totemic kangaroos (the sleeping places of living kangaroos are easily recognized by just such a pattern, worn by their tails in the soil). Aside from sticks used to beat out a rhythm and simple percussion devices such as tapping a stick against a spearthrower, the desert Aborigines have no musical instruments.

Among most of the Ngatatjara every person belongs to one of six named categories or "sections."[5] White Australians sometimes call these "skin groups." Sections serve to regulate marriage, and they play a vital role in enabling widely separated groups or individuals to visit one another. They serve as a kind of "shorthand kinship"[6] which allows visitors, even those with distant or nonexistent kinship ties, to participate in ceremonies, seek out potential marriage partners, and share food and other necessities while far from home. The names of the sections also serve on occasion as personal names. The operation of this so-called six-section system (really four sections with six names) has been accurately depicted by the Australian missionary and linguist Wilfred H. Douglas, in the diagram reproduced here.[7]

The "six-section" marriage system currently used by most Aborigines at the Warburton Ranges Mission.

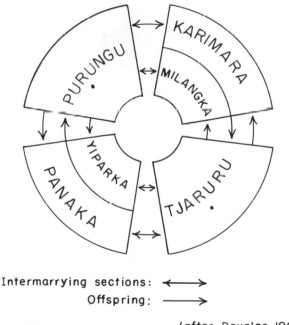

Intermarrying sections: ⟷
Offspring: ⟶

(after Douglas, 1964)

At Warburton, "wrong" marriages—that is, marriages violating this section system—were rare. Out of ninety-four marriages that Betsy and I recorded in our genealogies only three broke the rules. In all three cases, the people involved had come originally from the region around the Ernabella Mission, about 300 miles east of Warburton. Anthropologists sometimes speak of these rules as expressing "preferred" marriages, but at Warburton I think the word preferred is too weak to express the full strength of these rules.

When we first arrived in the desert, my wife and I were asked by the Aborigines what sections we belonged to. I named the first one that came to my mind, which was "Panaka," and Panaka I remain for the rest of my life. Consequently the only correct section my wife could belong to was Tjaṛuru (which she declared herself to be), and any children we may have will be Karimara. Anyone who enjoys logical and mathematical games would find it entertaining to fit all his relatives into this scheme. The Aborigines do so as a matter of course. Sometimes these sections are called "classes" by European and other scholars, but this word can be misleading, since it may imply social ranking, which emphatically does not occur among the desert Aborigines.

During the singing, men from different sections arrange themselves in the "sun" and "shade" circles[8] as shown in the following diagram:

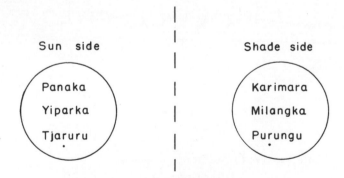

Seating of the "sun" and "shade" divisions during Kangaroo-cycle and other ceremonies.

Notice how generation-levels, marriage rules, and seating within the divisions are all correlated by this arrangement. This seating arrangement in opposed circles is conspicuous during the singing leading up to and during the circumcision ceremony. For other ceremonies the singers sit on different sides of the dance area but do not always form distinct circles.

The men performing and directing dances leading up to the final night belong to groups which the Australian anthropologist Mervyn Meggitt has aptly termed "cult-lodges." [9] Each of these groups consists of men who believe themselves to be descended in the male line from the same dreamtime being. Formally speaking, women are also members of these groups by virtue of descent, but they are not permitted to watch the dances or learn the sacred traditions. Instead, their male relatives act on their behalf at these ceremonies.

During the period leading up to the final rituals, sacred boards are brought out by the different cult-lodges from their respective caches and displayed to the other initiated men present. The incised designs are reverently contemplated as the lodge elders explain the story-lines depicted on each one. Sometimes additional paraphernalia, such as sacred stones and large pieces of incised pearlshell, are displayed at this time. They are then replaced in their respective caches.

The dances performed by the cult-lodges are moments in which the dreamtime past fuses with the present. The dancers feel a closeness of spirit with their totemic ancestors, becoming in the dance the being himself. At the conclusion of each dance a singer reaches out with his hand or a stick to touch a dancer, thereby breaking the spell and drawing the dancers back into the present.

Although short in themselves, these dances usually require several hours of preparation, mainly for decorating the dancers' bodies and the sacred paraphernalia carried or used in the dances. Members of each cult-lodge carry out these preparations with extreme care, with the older members supervising each detail and instructing younger members on the correct designs. While not as spectacular as the dance regalia seen in other parts of Aboriginal Australia, the preparations are thought by the Aborigines to be at least as important as the actual dances. This is not so much a matter of craftsmanship or artistry as propriety; that is, each design or piece of paraphernalia is judged by the older men in terms of whether or not it includes all the traditionally correct elements for the particular ceremony being performed. An appropriate design is called *ţulku mulapa* (true [or "proper"] sacred tradition). A neat, carefully painted body design is enjoyed by the lodge members but is not required for the ceremony. In short, craftsmanship and artistry are permitted and even, in an informal way, encouraged, but only if they do not in any way violate the themes set down by tradition.

Activity begins early on the final day. With such a large group present the excitement is intense. At dawn the women and children sit together near the camp, wailing. The men stand apart and sing. The entire scene is covered with a pale blue haze left by the still-smoking fires of the night, and the strong shadows caused by the rising sun create a shimmering quality in the air not matched at any other time of day. After the songs the women and children are chased away by the shouts of the men, who retire to the dance ground to meet with the novices.

Immediately upon arrival at the dance ground the men divide into two circles and begin singing sacred songs about the dreamtime Kangaroo (*Maļu*). The novices are made to lie down, and blankets (acquired from the Mission) are placed over them. They remain under the blankets throughout the entire day except for brief moments when they are told to sit up and watch dances. This is an occasion for high spirits and camaraderie. With much hand-gesturing and use of a complicated kind of "double-talk" used on ceremonial occasions,[10] the men in the different song circles jest about what will befall the novices later in the day. Some of the finger gestures are graphic and exaggerated portrayals of how the boys' penes will be operated on, and these never fail to bring howls of laughter. The big joke, of course, is that the boys under the blankets can hear the bloodthirsty note of glee in the men's voices but can only guess (too rightly, in fact) what is so funny.

One man, circumcised a few years ago, is carried away by the enthusiasm of the moment and declares that he will be subincised right now. He is quickly grabbed by several men (his

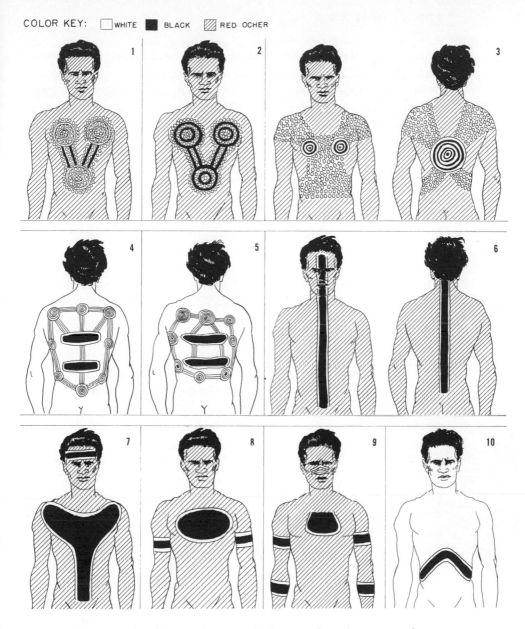

Body painting designs for sacred dances: (1, 2) connected waterholes on the track of the ancestral Carpet-snake, Tingari cycle; (3) kurrajong seeds, Tingari cycle; (4, 5) waterholes on Carpet-snake track, with two beating-sticks, Tingari cycle; (6) echidna (spiny anteater); (7) totemic Eagle, Tingari cycle; (8) totemic Kangaroo, Kangaroo and Dingo cycle; (9) totemic Dingo, Kangaroo and Dingo cycle; (10) sunrise, Kangaroo and Dingo cycle.

"brothers," both real ones and other men belonging to the same generation and section as himself) and held tightly as he is tilted backward, exposing his penis. The operator, an older man, steps forward and, using a sharp stone flake, cuts open the man's urethra from the meatus to a point about halfway to the scrotum. This is a fantastically painful operation, said to be even worse than circumcision, and the victim nearly passes out. But he sustains the entire operation without a murmur or cry and is quietly praised afterward for his fortitude. There is singing or other ritual attached to this operation. Afterward the victim stands close to a fire for a while to let the wound dry and then sits quietly off to one side for the rest of the day.

Meanwhile, other men have retired to a point in the bush where they cannot be observed directly. Using sharp, pointed sticks they reopen their own subincision wounds and line up in a semicircle on the dance ground facing the singers. They perform a series of hopping dances back and forth directly in front of the novices, while the blood from their penis wounds splashes on their thighs. Then they too stand for a while by the fires to let their wounds dry. Immediately following this series of dances, I noticed some younger men running individually among the song-circles. Each would dart in and stand in front of an older man, lifting him up under the arms and embracing him tightly. According to Tindale, who witnessed a circumcision ceremony among Pitjantjara Aborigines in South Australia, in this practice the younger man embraces the man who held his penis during his circumcision.[11] It is a mark of public courtesy and appreciation by the younger man and is expected of him on this occasion. This ritual is followed by another hopping dance involving freshly reopened subincision wounds and an episode in which each of the novices is taken by a group of his classificatory brothers and tossed into the air (I was told that this was to let everyone see the boys), while everyone else in the gathering wails. After this the boys are hustled back under their blankets and the singing resumes.

For a little while at least there are no more dances or other activities, and I take advantage of the lull to collect my thoughts and try to assimilate what I had just seen. Although I have read about the practice of subincision and watched films of it, the first direct exposure is a grim experience. I know that more of this sort of thing will follow, and I try to understand why these men are willing to subject themselves to such excruciating ordeals.

Further dances follow, all re-enacting episodes from the travels of the totemic Two Kangaroos in the vicinity of Mount Davies, a prominent landmark in South Australia, about 180 miles east of the Warburton Mission, which has many sacred associations. For these dances, ocher and charcoal pigments are liberally applied to the dancers' bodies and, as a final touch, blood is sprinkled over the shoulders, chest, and back of each dancer, using either penis blood or blood taken from the basilic vein in the arm. The final dance portrays the totemic Echidna. This animal is a desert monotreme with quills that make it look like a small porcupine. It sometimes protects itself by digging into the ground in a series of jerky movements which always leave its quills facing upward for protection, and the dancer on this occasion is widely renowned for his ability to mimic these movements. His performance elicits great glee from the singers and adds a lighthearted touch to the proceedings.

Once again there is a lull in the activities, though singing continues without interruption. Portions of a couple of kangaroos which were cooked and divided yesterday are shared and eaten, and many of the men relax or talk among themselves. The atmosphere at times like these is like that of a men's club, with banter and easy conversation among peers and attention and respect by younger men toward the lodge elders. This is generally the case whenever cult-lodges assemble to prepare for ceremonial events, and young men who have not been initiated yearn to join in the camaraderie of these gatherings. Meanwhile the women and children return to the main camp from their temporary camp in the bush, and everyone awaits sunset and the final phase of the ceremony.

On most evenings nightfall comes quietly in the desert, but not now. Big fires are lighted as the women and children assemble in the place where they sat this morning. The men walk over from the dance ground and stand waiting. About 200 people are present. There is an air of excitement, with shouting and laughter, as everyone waits for darkness to fall. When are things going to start? There is some confusion, as there often is when an important event is about to occur. No one is in a position of authority to start the ceremony. The lodge elders have declared their readiness to proceed, but, like everyone else, they do not wish to be thought of as "bossy," so they procrastinate along with the rest. As a rule, the excitement at times like this must be allowed to build up to the point where everyone is impatient to act. Then an assertive man knows that his "bossiness" will be overlooked in favor of general approval about what needs to be done—in this case the boys' circumcision. In this case, the lead is taken by a small group of classificatory elder-brothers of one of the novices. Since there is no official leader or governing body in Aboriginal society, it takes a while for the matter to be decided. At long last the initiated men form into two tight bunches, one for the sun group, the other for the shade, and start for the dance ground.

The men in each group alternately run and walk toward the dance ground, grunting or shouting in unison as they go. When they arrive, each group runs back and forth across the large clearing where the ceremony will take place, then sits down in its circle and starts singing. The women and children follow the men and sit together at one end of the clearing. As the singing continues, several women get up and perform a simple dance, hopping stiffly with their heads and arms hanging limp. As soon as they finish, about a dozen men assemble at the opposite end of the clearing about 100 feet away. The women and men all pick up burning sticks from the fires and, with much shouting and histrionics, hurl the firebrands through the air at each other. This causes a brilliant effect, like fireworks. After a few minutes, the women send some young boys running across the clearing to the men, who toss them into the air and make them run back in a line. Finally the men sit down and return to their singing.

One man remains at each end of the clearing to build up an enormous bonfire, then these men, too, return to the song-circles. For a while the gathering becomes quiet, except for the singing which grows less excited and more carefully cadenced. There is real tension at this point, with the women and children straining to see past the bonfires. Suddenly the three naked novices emerge from between the two fires, running in a line in perfect step with one another and with the rhythm of the singers. From a choreographic point of view this is a brilliantly engineered dramatic climax which would delight the most jaded ballet-goer. As the boys appear, the women and children begin to wail loudly, and before the boys reach the end of the clearing where everyone is seated, another electrifying sound is heard above the cries. A carved sacred board of medium size, called a bullroarer, is rotated rapidly through the air and as it spins it emits a weird, heart-stopping noise which is said to be the voice of the totemic Kangaroo. Even after I had seen this ceremony several times, the whir of the bullroarer always brought shivers up my spine. The effect on the women and children is dramatic—in a screaming mob they all run away from the dance ground and from the camp, back to their temporary camp in the bush.

Singing continues for a while as several men get up and perform a rapid backward dance with wildly vibrating knees. After they sit down, the two bonfires are built up, and again there is an air of expectancy. The bright glare of the fires acts as a curtain across the far end of the clearing. While the singing continues, a pair of unpainted naked men emerge, weaving back and forth across the clearing in a rapid, high-stepping dance. They skillfully control their movements in exact unison, and between them in an upright position is suspended a magnificent string cross constructed on an eight-foot spear. This piece of sacred paraphernalia is called *waniki*, and it is, for the duration of the ceremony, the actual body of the dreamtime Kangaroo. The novices see this exceedingly sacred item for the first time as they sit upright between the song-circles. The dancers pass swiftly in front of them, then zigzag their way back across the clearing and disappear behind the fires. Everything is done so expertly and happens so quickly that it hardly seems real. My subjective reaction to this episode was that at no other time I could recall did I feel more as if I had been in a dream while still awake, and I think this was exactly the dramatic intent of the performance. The action flowed silently, in perfect time with the rhythm of the singers, emerging out of the blackness between the fires at the end of the clearing and returning there, all in the space of perhaps thirty seconds. The absolute perfection of this presentation of the waniki was talked about among the men for weeks afterward.

Abruptly, the singing stops. A group of young men run forward and build a large bonfire, then settle themselves next to one another on their hands and knees to form a "human table" in front of it. One of the novices is picked up and carried by several of his *kuṭa* (elder brothers, real and classificatory) to the table. They lay him across it on his back. Another brother grips the boy's penis to keep it steady, and the operator (the novice's maternal uncle and also his potential father-in-law) steps forward. Still another brother draws the foreskin forward as far as he can. The operator then takes a stone knife and, either by slicing directly through or by cutting around a few times, removes the foreskin. A lad who has been troublesome as a youth or during his seclusion in novicehood may be punished at this time by prolonging the operation, but on this occasion and with the other two boys the operation proceeds without delay. The foreskin is passed to the boy's older brothers, who take it away and place it by the fire. If it wiggles while drying it is a sign that the boy will be unruly and a possible troublemaker (mainly in the sexual sense) as an adult. Then the dried foreskin is shared and eaten by the brothers. If the boy is mutilated during the operation, bleeds to death, or dies from an infection of the wound, these brothers have the duty of pursuing the circumciser and killing him. Meanwhile the boy is congratulated and led to the fire where he sits, letting the heat dry the wound.

Despite the intense pain, none of the three initiates cried out at any time. The ceremony is now over, and each novice, dazed from the operation, is quietly led away to a secluded place in the bush. Tomorrow the initiated men will meet with the novices in their camp and make sacred hair-buns (*pukutji*) which all of them, including the novices, will wear. While their wounds heal, the lads will remain in seclusion, wearing the hair-buns and keeping silent the whole time. The ordeal is over, and in several weeks they will return to camp as initiated men.

The traditional hair-bun
(*pukutji*) worn only after
circumcision.

Circumcision is but one of a series of physical ordeals that
young men must endure. It is usually preceded, without much
ritual, by knocking out an incisor tooth and the piercing of the
nasal septum and is followed by a fire-walking ordeal, chest-scari-
fication, and subincision. Circumcision is attended with more
ritual than the other operations (although the fire-ordeal runs a
close second) and also has the greatest importance. Each ordeal
is preceded by a period of instruction, sometimes perfunctory, as
is usually the case with tooth-evulsion and nose-piercing, but on
other occasions quite extensive, as with circumcision and the fire-
ordeal. Each ordeal marks a new plateau in the novice's position
within his cult-lodge. Totemic cult-lodges in some ways resemble the fraternal associations that most Americans are familiar
with. Each has a preliminary or major initiation (cicumcision in
the case of the Aborigines), along with a series of stages marked by
the acquisition of the further esoteric knowledge. In the Aborigines' case, even after the physical ordeals are finished, there are opportunities for acquiring sacred knowledge through visits to distant groups and discussions with lodge elders. Most men continue
to gain more and more such knowledge as they grow older, thus

becoming repositories of a large fund of this information in their old age. Hence lodge elders are consulted and deferred to in sacred matters, though not always in everyday life.

The Ngatatjara circumcision-ritual I have described is similar in general character and most details to circumcision ceremonies described for other Aborigine groups, and as a class these ceremonies are well known to anthropologists. At the time I witnessed my first I was too busy recording the details to give much thought to their meaning. Interviews and further opportunities to be present at ceremonies led me in time to the opinion that, in terms of their persistence in Ngatatjara culture, circumcision and other ordeals serve an essentially social function. This interpretation sounds prosaic when compared with those offered by other anthropologists. The European anthropologist Professor Arnold van Gennep stressed the death-rebirth symbolism of many of the rites connected with circumcision and other ordeals (for example, wailing, abandonment of the camp, and other behavior related to mourning).[12] Dr. Geza Róheim, a Hungarian anthropologist and psychologist, writing about fieldwork which he carried on in Central Australia in 1929, proposed an oedipal interpretation of circumcision by emphasizing the generational conflict between the circumciser (of the father's generation) and the novice (of the son's generation).[13] Dr. Ronald M. Berndt and Dr. Catherine H. Berndt of the Department of Anthropology at the University of Western Australia, in their analysis of circumcision among certain Arnhem Land tribes, point out that the removal of the foreskin symbolizes the final severing of the novice's umbilical connection with his mother and, along with this, a withdrawal from his former association with women.[14] These are useful and valid interpretations but pertain more to the symbolism or origin of the ritual than to its functioning role within the society.

The novice's entire social identity depends on his ability to withstand pain courageously and to absorb instruction in sacred matters during the periods marked by these ordeals. The novice knows this, and, as Tindale correctly observes, "The avidity with which the newly initiated youth enters into ceremonial life and the acquiring of the hidden significance of the mythological traditions and practices of the tribe is remarkable."[15] Although membership in a cult-lodge depends upon birth, it must be validated by circumcision and other ordeals before the novice will be admitted as an adult and responsible member. The circumcision ritual itself is part of the totemic kangaroo tradition which is shared by all Ngatatjara men, regardless of their particular lodge affiliations. But without this experience a man may not proceed to further stages of participation in his own lodge's affairs. When one realizes this fact, it is easier to understand why men who have already been circumcised volunteer for the further and even more painful ordeal of subincision. They are pressured into it, not so much by direct coercion as by the realization that to delay too long is to invite ridicule and insults about one's manhood and also to be excluded from ceremonies in which only subincised men may join. When asked about this, lodge members and novices alike are quick to point out the impossibility of any man's attaining social adulthood without enduring these trials. As social-psychologist S. D. Porteus pointed out in 1929, the physical wound is acknowledged as a badge of the initiate's increased ritual status and an emblem of his physical courage.[16]

This emphasis on a social interpretation agrees with that proposed by the Australian anthropologist and professor emeritus at the University of Sydney Dr. A. P. Elkin.[17] In addition to pointing out the social value of initiation rites to the novices themselves, Professor Elkin goes on to emphasize their importance to the society as a whole:

"It is almost impossible for those who have not witnessed such ceremonies, to realize the important part they play . . . in strengthening the unity and sense of common purpose in the tribe as a whole. Indeed, the very possession of great secrets, won as the result of a difficult journey through initiation on the part of all men of the tribe, helps to bind the tribe together and to counteract any disruptive tendencies which may arise from the localized character of much of Aboriginal social and spiritual life."[18]

I still did not understand, however, what makes the totemic cult-lodges so important. I could see that feelings of camaraderie along with pride in status and secret knowledge were significant motives for enduring the pain and humiliations of novicehood, but these did not fully account for the persistence of the cult-lodges or the overwhelming significance attached to them by the Aborigines. I needed to know more before the rituals connected with lodge-behavior would make sense to me.

Links to the Land

My first efforts to understand the meaning of cult-lodges in Aboriginal life led me toward the strictly practical. It was apparent that some aspects of Aboriginal ceremonies were closely connected with important parts of daily life. For example, the discipline of the novices during seclusion and the rigors of physical pain during initiation helped instill an ability to withstand pain and isolation in general, abilities useful to any people who must live by foraging in a chancy and sometimes hostile environment. Experienced observers, such as Australian Professor of Anthropology at the University of Adelaide, Dr. Theodor G. H. Strehlow, have noted the remarkable cheerfulness of the desert Aborigines even under harsh living conditions. Strehlow quotes his "civilized" Aranda guide as saying about the desert nomads near Mount Liebig in Northern Territory: "They are always laughing—they can't help it." [19] Often I have had cause to notice this same good cheer and readiness to laugh and joke among the people of the Gibson Desert, even when they are plagued by boils and heat, pestered by flies, and short of food. This cheerfulness seems to be part of a disciplined acceptance of frequent hardships which complaints would only aggravate.

Another practical value, suggested by Tindale, is in learning the names and locations of watering places through contact with the myths about them.[20] These are first learned by novices in the instruction given to them during initiations, both in songs and dances and from the designs inscribed on sacred boards. As mentioned earlier, the designs carved on decorated spearthrowers also play a part in this instruction. Long sequences of named water-holes are memorized along with the stories (told in song) of the dreamtime events that occurred in these places. Initiates also sometimes visit the places connected with the sacred traditions. In watching young men in such situations, I have been impressed by their earnest efforts to absorb every detail of instruction. Having previously memorized the songs about the place, the initiate looks around carefully to make sure that every detail of topography and vegetation also registers on his consciousness. Even while departing, from time to time he casts a glance back over his shoulder, "back sighting" on the waterhole so that he will recognize it if he returns. The usefulness of this kind of knowledge to the desert people is obvious, and the cult-lodges, with their ordeals and instructions, help foster its recall and its transmission from one generation to the next.

These examples show that Aboriginal ceremonial life is not cut off from the practicalities of subsistence and daily living, even though much of the ceremony and ritual takes place in isolated settings, away from women and children. But although the knowledge and discipline promoted by the sacred life are useful to the Aborigines, I found that in interviews my informants never consciously expressed these practical ideas to support their views about the importance of the totemic cult-lodges in their lives. Before long I realized that I was dealing as much with feelings or sentiments as with strictly practical motives. The experience that gave me the greatest insight into the particular emotional appeal of the sacred life was my trip to Pukara.

Pukara is a sacred waterhole about 135 miles east of the Warburton Ranges Mission, in rugged sandhill country a few miles south of the Bell Rock Range. We reached it in the morning after a particularly rough cross-country trip. The weather was hot, and the tires on the Land-Rover, riddled by stakes after months of this kind of driving, required constant patching and repair. I made the trip with four Aborigines who had expressed a desire to perform a series of important rites at this place. Three were Pitjantjara-speakers and the fourth a Ngatatjara-speaker who "switched" dialects temporarily out of respect for the others. Along the way we stopped at a place where a vein of red ocher was exposed among the rocks. One of the men ground some of the ocher into powder and mixed it with the fat of an emu that had been killed during the trip. With this dark red pigment he drew a series of parallel lines across his chest.

In situations like this I have found that it does little good to ask questions beforehand. It is better to watch what happens and afterward ask the senior lodge members to explain, which they are usually willing to do. At the time I can only keep notebook and camera ready in an unobtrusive way.

We rest at Pukara until around midday; then my four guides get up and start walking to the north in single file, away from the waterhole. I follow at the end of the line.

The group proceeds in silence between the sandhills for about a mile. As we cross one unusually high sandhill I can see the purple peaks of the Bell Rock Range in the distance, tantalizingly close yet blocked off by row upon row of bright pink sandhills. These peaks were given their English name by Ernest Giles in 1873 when he noticed the bell-like tones their rocks gave off as his iron-shod horses walked across them.[21] Tindale has recorded an instance where rocks in the Blyth Range not far away from here are rung by the Aborigines as part of their ceremonies.[22] The ringing sounds are said to be the "voices" or "talk" of the totemic ancestors, and I wondered if the rituals I was about to see would make use of "musical stones" in this manner.

Continuing our journey, we pass through a grove of mulga scrub and approach an area of low rocky formations between the sandhills. These rocky formations are covered with small desert mallee trees with long, pale green leaves hanging limp in the still, hot air. The rocks, probably sandstone of some kind, are pale yellow in color, and as soon as my guides see them they begin to wail loudly, kneeling and covering their eyes as they cry. This kind of wailing is fairly stereotyped behavior among the desert Aborigines whenever someone is sick or has died.

The wailing continues for about five minutes. Then the men quietly rise and walk over to a cluster of eight small rockpiles, all formed from the yellow rock in the nearby outcrops. The largest of these piles stands to a height of 21 inches and is about 5 feet in diameter. Each pile has a space around it which the men proceed to clear of weeds and pebbles. I notice, too, that there is a hearth next to each rockpile. The men go off for a few minutes and return with firewood. This they place on four of the hearths, with each man at a separate rockpile. A branch is split

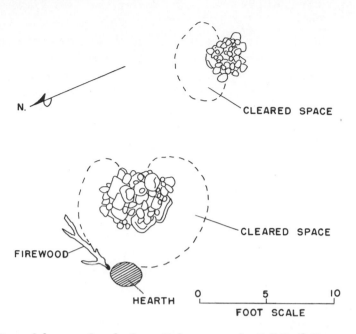

Two of the sacred rockpiles at Pukara, near the Bell Rock Range.

and placed on the ground and thin wedges are inserted to hold the crack open and "nail" the branch to the ground. One man stands astride the branch to hold it down, while another places bits of dry kangaroo dung in the crack and lays the edge of his spear-thrower across the branch at a point directly above the dry dung. He holds one end of the spearthrower and a third man kneels and takes hold of the other end. The two men saw vigorously back and forth with the spearthrower, working between the standing man's legs. In about twenty seconds a faint wisp of smoke appears from the dung inside the crack, and the men stop sawing and begin to blow on the smoldering dung, adding bits of dry grass to it as tinder. The faint glow spreads until the tinder is alight, and the burning tinder is then carried around to light the four fires.

Under nomadic conditions this is the only method the desert Aborigines have of making fire. Ordinarily, when I am traveling in the bush with Aborigines, I give them matches, but on this oc-casion I have used up my entire supply in vulcanizing tire-patches. Once on this trip, I even had to ask my companions to light a fire by this traditional method so I could make a tire-patch—one of the ironies that often occur when traveling in this region.

After lighting the fire, each man steps up to his rockpile and, using a small, sharpened stick, jabs at his subincised penis until the wound is reopened. When blood flows freely from the wound it is sprinkled over the rockpile. This accomplished, each man then stands for a few minutes by his fire to let the heat dry the wound and slow the flow of blood. These activities are carried on in a sober silence.

This completes the first part of the ritual, and the men form into single file and walk back to the waterhole, one of them carrying a firestick. Again, silence is maintained. The atmosphere throughout this episode is one of extreme reverence and meditation. From the time we arrived at the rockpiles the men have seemed deeply engrossed in contemplation, and I must be content with watching and recording what I see.

Back at Pukara, the man with the firestick uses it to ignite the dry brush surrounding the waterhole. In a few minutes all the brush and thorns that have accumulated since the place was last visited are burned off. The men stand around, contemplating the waterhole. They call me over and point out some of its features. The water smells vile, like marsh gas, and is black and oily in color. Nevertheless, the men find it drinkable. The waterhole lies in a natural depression or hole in a shelf of limestone at the edge of a dry lakebed. All around the lakebed are high sandhills, turning from pink to red as evening approaches. On the limestone surface at one side of the waterhole, there is a series of natural ripples or parallel grooves. These, I am told, are the chest scars of the totemic Waṇampi Kutjara (Two Water-snakes) who visited this place in the dreamtime. The man who painted his chest with red ocher explains that he and the three other men are members of this cult-lodge and that he is the oldest man present. The red ocher on his chest represents the chest scars of the Water-snake-men (human and animal forms are largely interchangeable in these myths).

We make camp on the broad crest of a sandhill about 100 yards from the waterhole. That night the men explain their behavior at the rockpiles. Pukara, they say, is where the Two Water-snake-men came in the dreamtime after collecting and eating large quantities of sweet yellow *wama*. They became sick at this place and vomited out the contents of their stomachs onto the ground. The wama they vomited out turned to stone (*yapuringu* —became rock [in the dreamtime]), becoming the piles of yellow rock where the men sprinkled penis blood today. The Water-snake-men accomplished this transformation "by themselves" (*yungara*), and today the spirit of these ancestral beings is alive and resides in the rockpiles.

The eldest man says that he and his son were both born near here. This place is their "dreaming," and he addresses his rockpile as "*ngayuku mama* [my father]"—meaning that he and his son both claim descent in the male line from the Water-snake spirit living within the rockpile. The three other men say that they were born at or near various other points along this same totemic track. Each of the other seven rockpiles is the paternal ancestor-spirit of a lodge member not with us on this trip, and the three men address the respective piles with kinship terms appropriate to their relationship to these absent members. Even though this place is not their own "dreaming" (that is, birthplace), as members of the same cult-lodge they have both the privilege and the duty of acting here on their relatives' behalf.

The wailing was a sign of sorrow over the illness of the totemic Water-snakes. The fires have no symbolic importance, but the sprinkling of penis blood is *kapi pinpa* (just like rain) in its importance in causing the actual grevillea flower—the source of wama, a highly prized and much sought-after delicacy—to ripen and the plants to multiply.

In short, all members of this cult-lodge, whether they have their actual "dreaming" here or act on behalf of relatives (including women) who do, have the sacred duty of performing this rite, annually if possible. By doing so they temporarily re-enter the dreamtime (hence the deeply meditative behavior during and after the ritual), and the rockpiles become part of their own being. Even when they are not performing the ritual, a direct kinship tie always exists between the men and the rockpiles. Their general duties as lodge members also include keeping the area around the rockpiles clean, seeing to it that the piles themselves remain intact, and, of course, deciding on suitable novices to instruct in the traditions.

Anthropologists commonly refer to rituals of this kind as "increase" ceremonies. Meggitt, however, has correctly pointed out that this term is something of a misnomer: "It is worth noting . . . that the term 'increase,' although commonly used in the literature in relation to such rituals, is not strictly accurate. The participants are simply concerned to maintain the supplies of natural species at their usual level, to support the normal order of nature."[23]

In this case, the members of the totemic Waṇampi Kutjara cult-lodge have acted to maintain the abundance of wama and regard the sprinkling of penis blood as an essential act in ensuring the ripening and continued fertility of this plant species. This ritual act benefits mainly the lodge members and their relatives, since these are the people who tend to forage and hunt in the general area around this sacred site, but it will also benefit any other people who may visit this region in search of food. Many "increase" ceremonies are also performed *in absentia* from the actual totemic site, generally when they are being shown to novices prior to an initiation ordeal.

At dawn the men get up and go directly to the waterhole. While one of them sweeps off the limestone shelf with an impromptu handbroom made of twigs and brush, the others climb into the water and begin removing handfuls of sticky black mud from the bottom. They splash around and laugh, obviously enjoying the mudbath. Now that the overgrowth is gone I can see a low embankment along the north side of the waterhole, and the men take their handfuls of mud and pile them on this mound. One takes a stick and starts poking around in the mud underneath the water. Soon he finds what he is looking for and begins lifting out pieces of smooth, naturally shaped rock and pieces of waterlogged wood and placing them on the swept area of limestone next to the pool. Forty-seven of these objects are dredged up and laid out to dry in the sun.

The work of removing mud from the waterhole is slow, but the embankment steadily grows higher until it stands almost 3 feet high and is completely coated with black slime. Meanwhile the pieces of stone and wood have dried and are being discussed by the men. They say that after recovering from their sickness at the site of the rockpiles the Two Water-snakes continued their dreamtime travels until they reached the present site of the water-hole. They entered the ground here, transforming themselves into the waterhole and also transforming various objects they had with them at the same time. They and these objects are said to reside in the waterhole today. Each of the pieces of wood and stone extracted from the mud is one of these transformed objects belonging to the Waṇampi Kutjara. The men point out one piece, a waterlogged stick, which they tell me is a piece of firewood belonging to the totemic beings. Another stick is the Water-snakes' wooden club (*kupulu*), and a piece of stone is one of their dogs. After being dried off and inspected, these objects are reverently replaced in the mud inside the waterhole.

Now the action proceeds rapidly. One man grinds a large quantity of red ocher and mixes it with water. Using his hand as a brush, he spreads the pigment over the rock rim of the pool, coating it thoroughly until the brilliant red color extends nearly all the way around (except for the spot below the mud-covered embankment). The other three men finish spreading the wet mud over the embankment and start inscribing serpentine designs in it, rather in the manner of fingerpainting. Before long the entire surface of the mound facing the waterhole is covered with these designs, which the men say represent the totemic Water-snakes. Pukara is now a spectacular sight. The black mud surface of the embankment, the bright red-ocher color of the waterhole rim, and the white of the swept limestone shelf combine to form a vivid contrast to the pale and dusty shades of the surrounding lakebed and nearby spinifex flats. It is an impressive transformation, and the men are proud of the results. In time, wind and rain will deface their handiwork, and vegetation will creep in and cover the site again, but the men have derived spiritual satisfaction from performing these acts and hope to return in another year to carry out their sacred duties once again.

After photographing Pukara for the last time and completing my notes, I load the Land-Rover and prepare for the trip back to Warburton. On the way, the men begin talking about their plans to come back. We have made this trip during the hot summer season, but they regard the ritual as more efficacious when held in the spring (September-October), shortly before the grevillea reaches full flower, and would like to come to Pukara at that time next year.

The anthropologists Ronald M. Berndt and Catherine H. Berndt point out that the myth of the totemic Water-snake, or, as it is often called, the Rainbow-snake, is widespread in Australia, particularly in Arnhem Land to the north and in the western and central deserts, where it is typically associated with rain and water.[24] For me, this ritual offered a firsthand awareness of something which the Berndts, Strehlow, and other scholars have mentioned in their writings—namely, the direct kinship ties which individuals have to particular sacred landmarks. These landmarks are nothing less than the bodies of the totemic beings, or items connected with them, transformed during the dreamtime into individual waterholes, trees, sandhills, ridges, and other physiographic features, as well as into rock alignments and sacred rock-piles, but still spiritually alive and influencing the present. The emotional sentiments of kinship are extended by the Aborigines to these sacred landmarks. Thus the sight of virtually every landmark, no matter how insignificant it may seem to the foreign visitor passing through the desert, brings deep emotional satisfaction to the Aborigine. No wonder Aborigines are able to find their way through this apparently featureless country, since their memories are constantly reinforced by spiritual ties with even the smallest rock outcrop.

An outsider might phrase this another way. The concept of the "dreaming" breaks down the separation of man and his physical environment. The desert Aborigines do not seek to control the environment in either their daily or their sacred lives. Rituals of the sacred life may be seen as the efforts of man to combine with his environment, to become "at one" with it. Deep feelings of belonging to a harmoniously ordered universe result from these apparently bizarre rituals, and a person's relationship to his "dreaming," carried on within the appropriate cult-lodge, becomes the core of his social and spiritual identity.

How to Get Rid of Ghosts

Not all Ngatatjara ritual is directly connected with totemic beings or with what I have termed the sacred life. While the Gibson Desert Aborigines are intensely concerned with totemic rituals, they also acknowledge the existence of a class of lesser spirits, the mamu which I mentioned in Chapter 1. Unlike the totemic beings, mamu can be coerced and even destroyed, mainly through the efforts of a sorcerer who possesses the appropriate magic.

Once when I was about to leave camp for a few days to collect some spearwood with three Ngatatjara men, a group of children told both me and my wife that the area around our tent was infested with mamu. The children knew that my wife would be alone for a while, and they were afraid that she might be attacked by these spirits. (The reader may recall that some Aborigines regard mamu as cannibalistic.) We decided to find out all we could about mamu before I left on my trip. While Betsy discussed mamu with the children and got them to make crayon drawings of what they thought mamu looked like, I interviewed some of the adult men, including Mitapuyi. Opinions about mamu differed, but some general points consistently emerged. For one thing, mamu are ghosts. This had already been pointed out by the Berndts, who noted that, after death, part of the deceased's spirit returns to its totemic spirit-center (the "dreaming" place), while the other part, the mamu, remains to haunt the living.[25] The mamu are night spirits, and many people we interviewed said that a low whistling sound in the bush indicated their presence. As I have mentioned, mamu are afraid of fire and can be seen by dogs. Only sorcerers can see them or their tracks and drive them away.

The attitudes toward mamu revealed by these interviews also helped us understand their role in Aboriginal life. Before long it became clear that one reason for the persistence of mamu fear is its use by adults as a "bogeyman" device, to scare young children into staying away from sacred places and to keep them from wandering away from camp at night. With children who do not yet understand *pika nguḷu* (the "danger of illness" from seeing or coming in contact with sacred paraphernalia, rituals, and so on), this is an effective disciplinary threat which is popular among parents, because it obviates the need to administer physical punishment. In our case, the children had been warned that mamu were plentiful in a sacred area near which our tent happened to be pitched. Because of our close proximity to this area, the children voiced concern for us, particularly since we did not have any dogs and did not keep a fire going all night.

Here was an opportunity we could not afford to let pass. I spoke to some of the men about the mamu near our tent, saying that we were worried about them, especially since I would be away for a few days, and asking if there were some way of driving them off. Mitapuyi replied that since he and his younger brother Tjun were both sorcerers, they would work together to rid us of mamu. (Later I learned that brothers often work together as sorcerers.) I agreed to pay for their services with tobacco, and we set off for my campsite.

At the insistence of the two men my wife leaves our campsite. At first I thought this was because of the separation of men's and women's rituals, but they assure me that it is mainly to limit knowledge in the camp about their magical techniques. Every sorcerer has certain individual techniques which he tries to keep as much as possible between himself and his client.

For about fifteen minutes Mitapuyi and Tjun stalk around our tent, looking in every direction. They return to where I am sitting and announce that we have not one but two mamu hovering near our camp; one they can see in the creekbed about 30 feet away and the other by a mulga tree where our waterbags are suspended. While they are showing me where they have spotted the mamu we walk over to the tent and, glancing down, I notice a bright flash of something on the groundcloth in front of it. I reach down and pick up a small, irregularly shaped piece of lustrous pearlshell (doubtless acquired in trade from the coast, hundreds of miles away). By sleight of hand, one of the men planted it here where I would be sure to see it. I ask about it, and I can see they have been expecting my question.

This piece of pearlshell and others like it are magical items (*mapanpa*) from the sorcerers' kits. They say they will use these bits of shell as magic projectiles to "shoot" the mamu. Mitapuyi sets off after the mamu by the tree while Tjun goes to the creek-bed after the other one. Each man moves slowly and with stealth toward his objective, stopping periodically to kneel and make a snappy arm-and-wrist motion which is clearly an act of "shooting" at the mamu. Pointing one arm in the direction of his target, each man clasps the outstretched forearm with the fingers of the other arm and then brings the clasping hand forward in a single sharp movement beyond the pointing hand. With this, the projectile is supposed to streak to the mamu and become lodged in its body, killing it. After about five minutes Mitapuyi stops and walks back to where I am sitting, but Tjun continues and soon is lost to view down the creekbed in a westerly direction.

At this point I ask to see the pearlshell again, but Mitapuyi tells me it is gone. He says it has wounded a mamu, as has Tjun's, and the mortally wounded mamu are fleeing to the west with the mapanpa inside them. They will die during the night, he says; then the pearlshells will fly through the air back into their kits. Tjun has returned by now, and both men agree that I may visit them tomorrow in their camps and see the pearlshells for myself.

Note the logic of this explanation. Naturally, the sorcerers hope their client is satisfied, and they have engineered the situation to prove to the client's satisfaction that their magic has worked. If one accepts the premise that these bits of shell really did fly through the air into the bodies of the mamu, then one must accept the further premise that they will fly through the air into the sorcerers' kits after the mamu die. Their presence in the kits tomorrow will "prove" that the offending mamu actually did die, and the client can stop worrying about them. (Needless to say, the men showed me the pearlshells a few days later.) As Dr. Max Gluckman and Dr. E. E. Evans-Pritchard, British social anthropologists who have worked extensively among African tribal societies, have demonstrated, magic and witchcraft can be carried out in an entirely logical manner within a consistent framework of cause and effect, only, of course, based on premises quite different from those of European logic.[26] There is no reason to think of magic, whether practiced by tribal Africans, Australian Aborigines, or anyone else, as illogical.

I told the men I was pleased with the results of their efforts and, as a last favor, asked that they each draw a picture in my notebook of the mamu they saw. Without hesitating for a moment or batting an eye each man in turn took my ball-point pen and quickly sketched a small, stick-like figure with a large, round head (see drawing below). As sorcerers, Mitapuyi and Tjun are practiced in the art of deception. Sucking cures, using deft sleight of hand to extract the "sickness"—in the form of an object from the sorcerer's kit—are common, and I have also seen designs painted by Mitapuyi inside a small cave near Partjar̲ which he says show the tracks he has seen left behind by mamu. Although I came to know Mitapuyi well during our stay in the desert, I never once heard him admit to any pretense in the realm of sorcery, though such pretense clearly occurs. Does a sorcerer sincerely believe in the magical system he uses? Or is he a charlatan with a very good line? I never learned the final answer.

In this case the situation was open to manipulation by the sorcerers. At other times, however, the results of a particular sorcerer's efforts cannot be manipulated, and his actions are open to scrutiny by the group. Such was the case at Warburton at 7:55 on the evening of October 26, 1966.

The two *mamu* (ghosts) drawn by Mitapuyi and Tjun.

The air is perfectly still. For me this is welcome, for the men are continuing into their second week of ceremonies, recounting events in the lives of Tingari,[27] a class of totemic beings whose dreamtime travels occurred about a hundred miles to the north, and on previous evenings it has been too windy for me to make really fine tape recordings of the singing. The songs in this myth cycle are particularly haunting and unusual, and tonight more than forty men, including eighteen novices, are present. I find it re-laxing to sit out in the desert with these men on nights like this, listening to their magnificent songs.

Suddenly the singing stops—the first and only time I ever heard a sacred song-cycle interrupted—and a couple of men point to the sky. Off in the main camp, about a quarter of a mile away, I can hear a loud hubbub and some wailing. Something extraor-dinary is happening. I can see a yellow cone-shaped streak of light high in the night sky. It looks like a fireball of some kind, but I cannot be sure.

There is no panic, but urgent discussion about what this light may be. Several men ask if it is a "whitefella" trick. (They were quick to notice artificial satellites when these first appeared.) I plead ignorance, and the discussion continues.

Old Tjupurula, a Ngatatjara man from the Rawlinson Range, suggests that the light in the sky is a mamu. His idea gets enthusi-astic support. A young Pintupi man (a desert Aborigine recently arrived at Warburton) steps out on the flat in front of the men and flails his spearthrower back and forth with a whirring noise. By this he hopes to drive the light away, but his magic fails. The fireball, or whatever it is, remains poised in the sky. The Pintupi sorcerer retires quietly after about five minutes, and two Ngata-tjara men (brothers from the Bedford Range, about 90 miles north of Warburton) walk out onto the flat to try their magic. These men have a wide reputation as sorcerers, so everyone watches them with interest. They begin by walking back and forth on the flat, stopping from time to time to peer at the light in the sky through old eyeglass lenses (acquired from whites somehow in the past). This "sighting" technique is a favorite of theirs; I have seen them use it in curing sick individuals. After about ten minutes of this they put the lenses back in their kits and start a new rou-

tine of scooping up handfuls of sand and throwing these in the
air at the light. Doggedly they keep at it. One of them stops hurl-
ing sand and starts the same snappy arm-and-wrist action I saw
used by Mitapuyi and Tjun. After about fifteen minutes of their
combined efforts, the light begins to fade. There is a quiet murmur of relief through the crowd and the two sorcerers sit down
as soon as the light has disappeared.

In this case the sorcerers appear to have believed sincerely
in the efficacy of their magic. They were willing to put their rep-
utations on trial, and, as luck would have it, they succeeded. The
earlier failure was largely forgotten in the quiet enthusiasm over
the success of these two men. Old Tjupurula said they were "*mapantjara mulapa* [real sorcerers]," and his broad grin showed
both his relief at their success and his pleasure at being the one
who correctly identified the unknown light as a mamu. Anti-mamu
magic drove it away, he reasons, so it must have been a mamu.

It was amazing good luck for me that I was present when
this event occurred. How many times in the past have such un-
expected situations arisen, with no one to record the response or
outcome? The Aboriginal belief in mamu-spirits and sorcery was
strengthened by this episode, and I am certain that the two sorcerers' techniques will be taken seriously for a long time to come.
From an objective standpoint, sorcerers who fail are usually ignored, while sorcerers who succeed—whether by pure luck, cal-
culated risk, or a degree of manipulation—are praised and their
magic sought after.[28] The relatively few successes do more to
strengthen belief in sorcery in general than the many failures do
to weaken it. What was the light in the sky? Even after checking
with astronomers, I do not know. I cannot argue with anyone who
wants to claim that it was a mamu.

6

Artists and Monuments

While my wife and I were passing through England on our way to Australia, we went with some friends to visit Stonehenge, the monumental rock alignment on Salisbury Plain. So much had been written and conjectured about this place that I feared the actual sight would be anticlimactic. My fears were groundless, for Stonehenge has kept its mysteries and continues to invite speculation.

Scientific archaeology has proposed numerous theories about the construction and purpose of Stonehenge, some of which, such as ingenious and quite plausible explanations of how the massive lintels were raised[1] and the interpretation of Stonehenge as an ancient astronomical observatory,[2] are compelling in their logic and careful use of evidence. Yet, interesting as they are, these theories are based on inference, since no historical accounts of Stonehenge in the days of its glory are available. Failing such evidence, there is room for debate—and not among scholars alone.

Some people still hold the older ideas that Stonehenge was built by Merlin or by the Druids and that it was a place of human sacrifice.

The magnificent Upper Paleolithic cave paintings of Europe have also aroused speculation and today are the focus for intense scholarly debate. The interpretations—once widely accepted—of the paintings as a form of sorcery or magic used in hunting are being challenged by ingenious theories put forward by the French archaeologist and Professor of Ethnology at the University of Paris (Sorbonne), André Leroi-Gourhan.[3] In classifying the paintings in scores of caves in France, Dr. Leroi-Gourhan has proposed that they are arranged in definite groupings within each cave which suggest an overall pattern of organization. He interprets particular animals and abstract signs as representations of either the male or the female principle, with the pattern of their positioning reflecting a coherent mythology based on the complementary opposition of the sexes.[4] This is an imaginative and revolutionary new approach to a long-debated subject, and it is too soon to predict the final outcome of the arguments thus generated.

No matter how these debates are resolved, studies of rock painting and rock alignments in living and historic societies can certainly make useful contributions to the discussion.

Both professionally and personally, I had wanted for a long time to see the art of rock painting and the use of rock alignments in a living society, and one of my reasons for choosing to study the desert Aborigines of Australia was the hope that these practices survived among them. More than any other living society of hunter-gatherers, these people seemed to offer an opportunity both to observe subsistence and daily life and to learn about monumental and rock art. With this in view I sent letters to anthropologists who had worked in Australia, but the initial reports I received were not encouraging. Several doubted that there were any nomadic Aborigines left at all, and the idea of their still practicing rock art was dismissed as unlikely. At first it looked as if I might be too late.

My only strong encouragement came from Professor Ronald M. Berndt. He not only informed me that such opportunities still existed but indicated specific places where useful research could be carried out. Everyone I had written to previously had agreed about what research should be done, but only he stated unequivocally that it could be done. Moreover, his advice was based on many years of firsthand anthropological work in the desert regions of Western and South Australia.

Once we were actually on our way, my wife and I knew that we were irrevocably committed to this venture. Our visit to Stonehenge in the winter of 1966 aroused mixed feelings of excitement and apprehension. Would we arrive in Australia in time to see the stone monuments of the desert Aborigines still in use? Would it be possible to see Aborigine artists making rock paintings? Or would the monuments and paintings of these Aborigines keep their mysteries as Stonehenge and the European cave paintings have done?

The Silent Rocks of Lake Moore

Our encounter with Aboriginal monuments came by stages. The first was at Lake Moore, a large dry lake about 230 miles northeast of Perth, Western Australia. This was not the region in which we planned to do our main studies, but a chance conversation at a pub in the tiny settlement of Payne's Find led us to make a detour to Mount Gibson Station, a large sheep ranch not far from Lake Moore where there was said to be an impressive rock alignment. We were greeted by the managers, Mr. and Mrs. Murray Andrews, who directed us in our Land-Rover over a difficult track to the lakebed.

A salt crust as smooth and white as fresh snow extended about seventy miles from north to south and about 3 miles from east to west, at the point where we approached the alignment. Except for the sounds of hot wind rushing off the lakebed and of birds in the early morning and evening, the place was profoundly silent. It was easy to imagine that no man had ever been here, yet here were these remarkable stones. About 50 feet out from the lakeshore stood a serpentine alignment over 200 feet long consisting of 437 rock slabs standing upright and 91 others which had fallen over in place. The individual rocks were small, most being less than 2 feet high, but the sight of the entire construction on the salt crust was impressive and haunting. Extending from the shore were remains of four smaller alignments, each one straight but poorly preserved. In the shoreline cliff directly opposite the southernmost of these small alignments was a small man-made cave consisting of long rock slabs laid side by side to form the roof to a crevice in the cliff.

My wife and I spent three days at the site, mapping and photographing the alignments, the cave, and the spring and camp-site which we discovered on the shore slope nearby. Although small cairns and rock patterns left by the Aborigines are encountered fairly often in this part of Western Australia, this was the most spectacular one we had seen or heard of. Naturally, we wondered what it had been intended for.

During the heat of the day we would "shade up" inside the Land-Rover, there being no shade available anywhere else nearby. Several times on the first hot afternoon we noticed emus emerging around a rocky promontory about 300 feet south of the spring where we were camped. These birds stepped out into a 20-foot wide gap between the small artificial cave in the promontory and one of the smaller rock alignments. Coming through this gap, they walked toward us until they saw the Land-Rover. Then they immediately turned and fled back through the gap and behind the promontory. This occurred several times, but at first we did not attach any significance to it. The next morning, however, we noticed dozens of kangaroo and emu tracks in the soft salt crust, showing that animals had come around the same way, through the gap, and approached to within about 150 feet of the spring. At this point they must have spotted us, for the tracks turned around and retreated back through the gap.

Here at last was a clue to the way these alignments may have been used. The relationship of the cave and the southernmost alignment suggests that this was a sophisticated game trap. A man could have waited inside the artificial cave, ready to spear emus or animals coming for water. These would avoid the upright rocks of the alignment by moving through the gap, in the way we had just seen the emus do, thus passing close enough to the cave for an easy shot with a spear. If the hunter missed, he could move into the gap himself, blocking it and chasing the bird or animal toward the spring where other men could be waiting. The other straight rock alignments would have had the same purpose of deflecting the game toward the spring or out onto the bed of Lake Moore, where they would become bogged in the slimy brown mud just beneath the salt crust.

In terms of the layout of the site this interpretation made sense. But it was based entirely on inference, as are archaeological interpretations of European monuments and cave art. Nor did it explain the main feature of the site, the serpentine alignment. We still wanted to know more about the place, and the only way was to find some Aborigines from this area and interview them.

For several days we visited different sheep ranches and native reserves. We found that most of the Aborigines of the Lake Moore region either had died or had lost their traditions many years ago, after prolonged contact with whites. However, I was able to interview separately three elderly men, who said they belonged to a group that they called Yungara, which once lived near this place. Yungara does not seem to have been a tribal name, though early historical sources for the area list this word both for the people themselves and as meaning "kangaroo." [5] Later we learned that the Gibson Desert Aborigines use this same word to mean "themselves" or "by themselves." The accounts the three Aborigines gave me about the site agreed closely and fitted the general pattern known for Australian Aboriginal sacred sites.

They agreed on the name of the place, pronouncing it variously as Kunturu or Kunturin. One of these men translated Kunturin as "something bunched up." The name probably refers to the curled pattern formed by the large alignment. They all said that this was an important ceremonial site which was visited both by local Aborigines and by people from farther east, who reached it by crossing the lake along a hard trail on the lakebed. This trail is visible today and leads directly to the site. The informants all explained that the dreamtime Water-snake (here called *Pimara*) came across the lake at this place, leaving the trail behind as his track. He turned into the large stone alignment and his spirit resides inside the freshwater spring nearby.

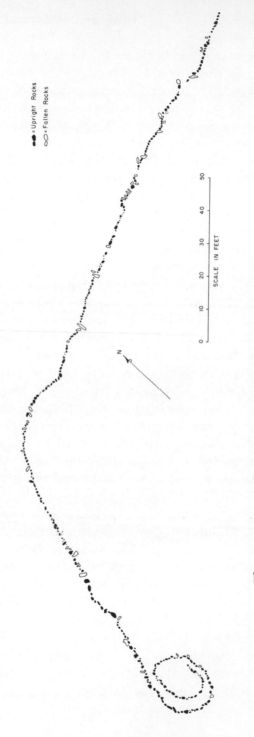

The serpentine rock alignment at Kunturu, Lake Moore, Western Australia (scale plan).

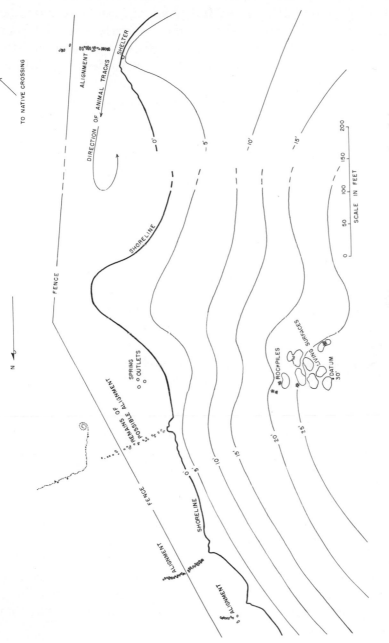

Contour map of the Kunturu site (alignment shown in reduced scale).

This was an interesting interpretation. In terms of what is known of the traditional culture of the region it has a ring of authenticity, though there is no independent way of testing the accuracy of the account. Although the interviews added to our understanding of the site, the state of Aborigine traditions still fell short of the high hopes we had set for our studies in the desert farther east.

From Lake Moore we drove to Laverton, a virtual ghost town left over from the gold-rush days of the early 1900s. There is a large Aborigine reserve close to Laverton, and, after three months of preliminary study there, we headed for the Warburton Ranges, where we hoped to find rock alignments which were still in use.

Kawan-kawan's Progress

The time we spent in the vicinity of Partjar, in the Clutterbuck Hills, while providing a close view of daily life among the Aborigines, also enabled me for the first time to see a large and important rock alignment actually in use. All the uncertainties about what we would find in the desert were resolved one morning when Minmara and Mitapuyi invited me to go with them into the canyon at Partjar.

This invitation was not accompanied by any explanation about what to expect. All I knew was that Partjar had a wide reputation as a sacred site on the track of the totemic Marsupial-cat called Partjata. On previous occasions I had walked only short distances up the canyon, but this time we proceeded farther, stopping from time to time for the two men to explain the sacred traditions of the place. This was my first direct exposure to the wealth of minute detail connecting the sequence of stories in a sacred myth to features of local geography, and I must admit to having had feelings of immense glee as the richness of the narrative unfolded during our walk up the canyon. Here was both the end and beginning of a quest. The search for people who actually used stone alignments had ended, and the quest to understand how and why they are used had begun.

The men said that in the dreamtime a war-party (*warmaḻa*) of totemic Marsupial-cat-people stopped here on their way to Yakuri, another site in the Clutterbuck Hills. During their stay at Partjaṟ an old man in the party circumcised a novice named Kawan-kawan ("standing up"). The story-line proceeded up-canyon, from north to south.

About 100 yards from the canyon entrance there are some small natural depressions in the bedrock of the creek. These marks were left by the buttocks of the novice as he sat waiting to be carried forward for his circumcision. Immediately east of this spot there is a small side-canyon where Marsupial-cat-men stood, out of sight, twirling bullroarers to keep women and children from the scene. A little farther up-canyon are two upright slabs of rock, each about 2 feet high, on opposite sides of the gorge, marking the beginning of the runway along which the novice was carried to be circumcised. The rocky slopes on the east side are men of the "sun" side; the rocks on the west are men of the "shade" side —separated just as the two groups are when singing before the real operation. The clearing or runway itself is the billabong at the bottom of the canyon, and in a rock face on the west slope immediately overlooking this sheet of water there is a natural crevice said to be the meatus of the novice's penis. A tall ghost gum at the end of the billabong is the novice himself.

Still farther up-canyon, there is an upright slab of rock about 24 inches high, supported by a circle of smaller stones around the base. This is the first of a series of 23 similar upright slabs, ranging from 12 to 30 inches in height and standing at irregular intervals in a row that extends about 1000 feet farther up the canyon. Included in this series is a cluster of about a dozen upright slabs along the east side of the canyon. Following the line made by these upright rocks, we arrived at a small gravel flat on a terrace just east of the creekbed. Out on the flat stood a 110-foot-long rock alignment containing 436 rocks, 39 of them upright. I made this count after each of my guides had approached a collapsed rock and placed it upright. Mitapuyi addressed his as *"ngayuku mama* [my father]." Although I later saw this kind of behavior many times at other sites—for example, with the rock-piles at Pukara, as described in Chapter 5—this was my first experience of it. Mitapuyi and Minmara then spent about twenty minutes clearing away the weeds and rubble which had accumulated around the rocks of the alignment since their last visit.

Later I returned and mapped the alignment, but at the time I was anxious to learn the meaning of the rocks. The men explained that the upright rocks in the alignment as well as those leading up to it were the totemic *pukutjitjara* (those who have hair-buns). The reader may recall that after a novice has been circumcised, he wears for the first time in his life a hair-bun (*pukutji*) bound up with hair-string. Previously circumcised men also wear their hair-buns at this time. The hair-bun is sacred and is worn only in the seclusion of the bush, never in camp. Thus the upright rocks are the totemic Marsupial-cat-men wearing their hair-buns following the novice's circumcision. The only exception is a large upright rock at the north end of the alignment, which stands 16 inches high, and has an irregular stripe of red ocher around it just below the top. This rock is Kawan-kawan's circumcised penis, the ocher being the blood from the fresh wound.

As in other cases I observed later, the meaning of the rock arrangements and the natural features surrounding them was so closely tied to specific details of the totemic mythology as to defy any interpretation by inspection. Just looking at these rocks, without the benefit of instruction by members of the appropriate cult-lodge, would never bring this kind of information to light. But, as this and other cases showed, a more generalized but still useful interpretation would be possible in situations where Aborigine behavior can no longer be observed. Rock alignments and artificial rockpiles are consistently interpreted as the bodies or paraphernalia of totemic beings changed by themselves into lithic form.

These alignments do not, of course, rival Stonehenge in their size or complexity of arrangement. Nor at this time do archaeologists know when the Aboriginal alignments were first constructed. The Ngatatjara say that these were not man-made but were all created by dreamtime beings. There are still mysteries to be solved in connection with these stone arrangements. But their general meaning is now much clearer, and other stone alignments in Australia probably share it. The serpentine alignment at Lake

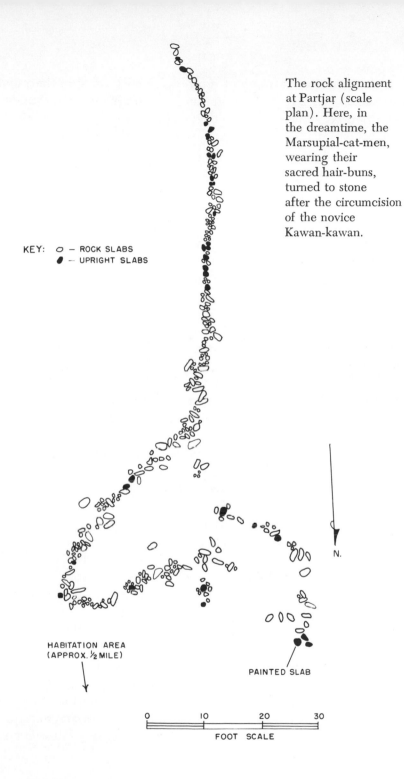

The rock alignment at Partjaṛ (scale plan). Here, in the dreamtime, the Marsupial-cat-men, wearing their sacred hair-buns, turned to stone after the circumcision of the novice Kawan-kawan.

KEY: ○ — ROCK SLABS
◖ — UPRIGHT SLABS

N.

HABITATION AREA
(APPROX. ½ MILE)

PAINTED SLAB

0   10   20   30

FOOT SCALE

Moore fits this general frame of reference, and I am sure that, as the archaeological exploration of Australia continues, many more such formations will be discovered.

Aborigine Artists

The eastern half of the Rawlinson Range (that is, east of the place named by Giles the Pass of the Abencerrages) is deeply indented by narrow gorges, several of which are veritable galleries of Aboriginal rock art. It was in one of these that I first encountered both paintings left by Aborigines and the artists themselves at work.

In those first months after leaving Laverton I had looked around the Warburton Ranges for signs of rock art but with little success. While other studies progressed well, this continued to be a source of frustration. Published accounts from farther east, most notably Australian anthropologist Charles P. Mountford's descriptions of the rock paintings at Ayers Rock and Mount Olga,[6] led me to believe that rock painting must in all likelihood exist in the Gibson Desert, too. (Later I found in several localities near the Warburtons rock paintings and even some rock engravings, but at the time I did not know of these.) Having failed thus far, my wife and I decided to look farther afield. With a personable and somewhat Westernized Ngatatjara guide named Paul Porter we drove the Land-Rover to the Rawlinson Range on the first of several extensive and rewarding visits to this place. Since most of the paintings were in places of totemic significance, Betsy had to remain in camp while Paul and I entered the gorges.

The first we visited, and by far the most impressive, was the great gorge at Wi:ntjara,[7] called Glen Cumming by Ernest Giles.[8] Because of its depth and narrowness, the bottom of the gorge is in nearly perpetual shade. This allows large pools of fresh rainwater to remain even during the hottest months, and the place is known to the Aborigines as one of the most dependable water sources in the region. There is nothing in the Warburton Ranges or in the sandhill country to compare with these magnificent gorges. Only to the east, in the Walter James and Petermann ranges, at Mount Olga, and in some of the ranges in South Australia are there deep, well-watered canyons like these. Shadowy, silent except for the sounds of dripping water and an occasional bird, these gorges give relief from the fierce midday glare and heat outside. The moisture at the bottom supports a profusion of vegetation, including large amounts of mingkulpa, the coveted native tobacco. Giles, during his visit to Wi:ntjara in 1874, remarked on the water but did not mention rock paintings. Either there were none there then or he failed to see them—probably the latter.

I did not see them at first either, mainly because the ones near the entrance to the gorge are on exposed rock faces where weathering has caused them to erode and fade. However, when I looked at them in shade it was possible to see the details clearly. It is ironic to think now that as the guide and I first looked at these faded paintings on that morning, we were unaware that, not a hundred yards from where we stood, two Aborigine men were painting a sacred design on a rock face near the entrance to a small cave opening.

They were as surprised as we when we met them later in the day. One was a Ngatatjara man who had lived at Warburton for a couple of years but had left the Mission about a month before to do some hunting in his home country and to visit again the places near his "dreaming." The other was a Pintupi man freshly arrived from the country around Lake Macdonald to the north, who called himself Kunmanara (the circumlocution used to avoid using a name similar to that of someone recently deceased). When we met them they were putting the finishing touches on an elaborate painting, intended, they said, to represent a type of sacred board called *kuṇṭala*. They used the simplest of pigments: crushed charcoal mixed with saliva, and kangaroo dung (applied dry, to give a dark yellow-green color). They explained that the concentric circles in the design were waterholes where the totemic Carpet-snake (Tjikaṛi) stopped as he crossed the desert to the north of here. The Carpet-snake is one of the class of totemic beings called Tingari who passed through the Gibson Desert in the dreamtime.[9] The lines connecting the concentric circles represent the Carpet-snake's track, and the

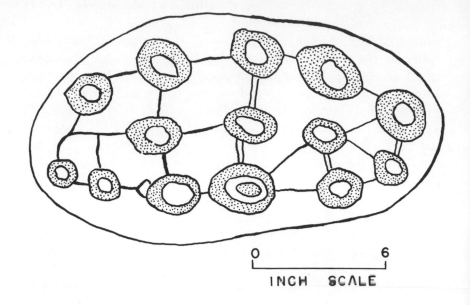

0   6

INCH SCALE

The *kuṇṭala* (sacred board) painted by Kunmanara on the rock face at Wi:ntjara (Glen Cumming) in the Rawlinson Range.

roughly oval-shaped line encircling the painting is the outline of the sacred board.

Wi:ntjara is a sacred place where the totemic Penis (Yula) pursued the Seven Sisters. He extended his penis toward the women here, splitting the cliff face while trying to reach one of them with it. Both of the men we met there belong to this cult-lodge. In the cave behind their painting, near the place where Yula is said to have split the cliff, there is a spring with water dripping continuously from the ceiling in the rear. This water, they said, is Yula's semen. Following this episode, Yula resumed his pursuit of the Seven Sisters, following them to the east as far as Wangkarin in the Petermann Range, where the tradition ends.[10] At Wangkarin, too, there are many fine rock paintings as well as several important totemic landmarks.

One thing puzzled me, however. If Wi:ntjara was sacred to Yula and the Seven Sisters, why were the men painting a design appropriate to a different myth? Later, while I was examining the other rock paintings there in the company of these men, this same question arose. Some of the designs pertained to the Yula tradition, but the majority involved other, mainly Tingari, traditions —those of Lungaṭa (the Blue-tongue lizard) and Nganuṭi (the Bush-turkey or Bustard). This pattern was repeated at many other sites which I visited later. Paintings pertaining to one tradition often appeared at sites which were sacred to other traditions. Landmarks, rock alignments, and rockpiles have immutable associations with sacred traditions, but paintings, though also sacred, can be altered. Although I never found out exactly what motivated the two men to paint Tingari designs at Wi:ntjara on that occasion, eventually I understood that paintings are man-made representations of sacred subjects and hence open to a degree of human manipulation. Landmarks and alignments, however, are the actual bodies of the totemic ancestors themselves. Any attempt to tamper with these or to alter their appearance would be sacrilege and would provoke an immediate hostile reaction from the members of the cult-lodge concerned.

This attitude may explain seemingly unprovoked attacks by desert Aborigines on some of the early explorers—for example, that on Giles' party at Fort Mueller in the Cavanagh Range, mentioned in Chapter 2. Since the Gibson Desert Aborigines are generally not warlike, such an attack is a rare event. What could have instigated it? Only a short distance from the site of Fort Mueller, there is a rock alignment, situated in a mulga grove, which contains 135 rocks, 48 of them upright. These are the transformed bodies of the totemic Opossum (Wayuṭa), and the rocky ridges surrounding the place (called Katangara by the Aborigines) contain natural outcrops also said to be totemic Opossums. Were the Aborigines who attacked Giles and his men members of this cult-lodge who feared that the white men would desecrate their sacred "dreaming" place?

Once I understood this basic distinction drawn by the desert Aborigines I could begin to appreciate the finer details of their mural art. Most of the designs appearing in caves or on rock surfaces depict subjects related to the sacred life. Specifically, they are drawn from the repertory of designs used by various cult-lodges to paint the bodies of novices and dancers at totemic ceremonies. Often my guides would point to a rock painting and

name a particular part of the human anatomy. At first this did
not make sense to me, since the designs did not look at all like
parts of the body. Later, after I had watched a number of different ceremonies, I realized that this was simply a shorthand way
of telling me what part of the dancer's body this particular design was applied to. These are mainly geometric patterns, the
most commonly used being concentric circles with lines connecting them. Ultimately these refer to sacred waterholes along the
dreamtime track of a particular totemic being. The other major
theme of the sacred rock paintings is the representation of paraphernalia used by totemic beings. At Wi:ntjara, for example,
there are several paintings representing large sacred boards
(*lara*) used by the dreamtime Tingari people. At Kalkakutjara,
an impressive rockshelter about forty miles from the Warburton
Mission, there are vivid paintings representing the sacred string
cross (*waniki*), the boomerang, and the wooden club used by the
totemic Two Men (Wati Kutjara). And at Mularpayi, about fifty
miles east of Warburton, there is a complicated pattern intended
to show the sacred hair-string belt (*nanpa*) belonging to one of
the Tingari beings.

Many of these designs appear in brilliant shades of red, yellow, and white ocher, with charcoal for black. These pigments
are mixed with emu fat as a fixative and if applied to a sheltered
rock surface (for example, inside a cave or deep crevice), will
last indefinitely. But because old designs are not venerated as
sacred in and of themselves, one generally finds the desert Aborigines partly obliterating the older designs with new ones. They
make no effort to "touch up" or freshen old designs the way
Aborigines in other parts of Australia are reported to do.[11] They
do not look upon the partial destruction of an earlier painting—
even of one representing a sacred theme—as sacrilegious. With
the passage of time, a rock surface can become a palimpsest of
superimposed paintings.

Sacred designs dominate the rock art of the Gibson Desert
Aborigines. Because of their geometric character, these designs
are not easy for the outside observer to understand. Although
every Aborigine knows, for example, that concentric circles usually indicate water sources along the track of a totemic ancestor

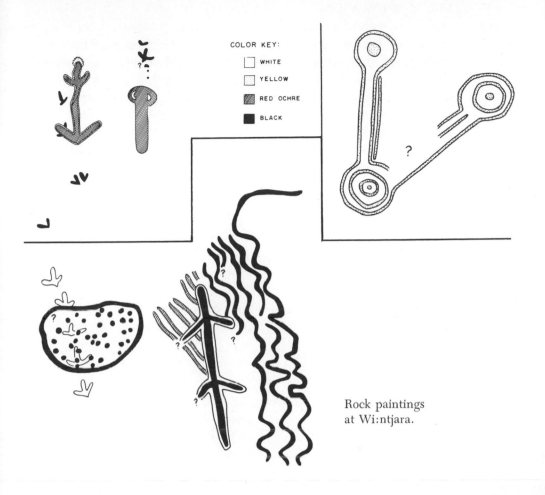

Rock paintings
at Wi:ntjara.

and that the connecting lines represent the track of the ancestor during his dreamtime travels, only the artist and his lodgemates know exactly which ancestor is being portrayed and the names and locations of the waterholes he visited. In other words, the specific meaning of the designs is part of the esoteric knowledge cultivated by each totemic lodge.

Certain sacred designs are believed to have been the work of the dreamtime totemic beings. Travelers in the Gibson Desert sometimes encounter rock engravings, generally of circles and concentric circles. The desert Aborigines today do not make rock engravings, and they regard them, along with sacred landmarks

and rock alignments, as transformed totemic beings. The concentric and plain circles found engraved at Wintjaru, a waterhole
about twenty-six miles north of the Warburton Mission, were
said to be the decorative patterns painted by the totemic Two
Men on the bodies of novices before showing them some sacred
dances. These designs turned to stone, where they appear today.
This case parallels another reported in 1966 by Robert Edwards,
an anthropologist from the South Australian Museum in Adelaide,
who found similar engravings on the rocks at Tukulnga, a rock-
hole in the southwestern part of Northern Territory. The Pitjantjara-speaking Aborigines that Edwards interviewed declared
that these designs had been left by the totemic Emu-people in
the dreamtime.[12]

Not all designs are sacred, however. A common theme in
rock painting is the depiction of animal tracks, particularly those
of kangaroos, wallabies, and emus. As I pointed out earlier, the
desert Aborigines are particularly "track-conscious" from their
earliest childhood, so it is not surprising to find tracks a popular
theme in their art. What is interesting is the fact that in nearly

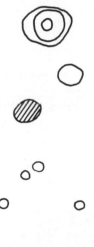

A few of the rock engravings at Wintjaru, near the Warburton
Ranges. Hatching indicates area that may once have served for
grinding seeds.

every case these designs are found in crevices, behind rocks, or next to a natural defile within easy spear-throwing distance of a water source. As my guides explained to me on several occasions, these track designs were put there by hunters as they waited in concealment for game to arrive. They were, in fact, a loose form of hunting magic. The men drew these designs because they were "thinking about meat." The act of painting was intended to hasten the arrival of their quarry. These designs are not sacred, nor are occasional designs in caves and other places depicting a hunt or an animal "just for fun."

In all, the survey that my wife and I carried out netted eighteen Aboriginal sites with rock paintings and two with rock engravings. In several instances we were the first whites to visit these places. Our discussions with Aborigines make it clear that many more such sites exist in the Gibson Desert, awaiting discovery. What emerged for me from these studies was both a personal and scholarly appreciation for Aboriginal rock art. The sight of the two men that first time, singing softly to themselves as they applied their pigments to the rock surface, is a scene which goes back in time to the earliest beginnings of this kind of painting, thousands of years ago, in the caves of Europe and elsewhere. Beyond that, however, was the awareness that this art possesses a kind of "grammar" of style, with orderly rules that distinguish different kinds of sacred and nonsacred designs.[13] The discovery of these basic attitudes on the part of the Aborigines toward their mural art proved the most rewarding part of the study. It added another dimension to my understanding of the sacred life led by each Aborigine.

No one knows how old the art of rock painting is in Australia, and the same can be said for rock engraving. Most scholars presume that these forms of Aboriginal mural art are extremely ancient, perhaps going back in time to the earliest human settlement of the continent. Using various techniques, archaeologists hope to answer this question one day. But though we do not know exactly when this art began in Australia, we do know when it will end—and that is soon. The results of white contact have been many and far-reaching for the Aborigines, and the start of settled life on reserves and missions signals the beginning of the end for this ancient mode of artistic expression. In one or two generations rock painting will probably have ceased altogether.

Why should this be? Most of the older Aborigines living in settlements like the Warburton Ranges Mission have the knowledge necessary to paint these designs, and, in addition, they have the desire to do so. Many of the younger men also continue to absorb the sacred traditions and learn the appropriate body designs that form the models for the rock paintings. The answer is that life on or near white settlements has created a set of circumstances that is qualitatively different from anything these people experienced during their nomadic lives in the desert. For one thing, the reserves and missions are simply too far from many sacred sites for the people to get back to them easily or even at all. But the reasons go deeper than that. Once exposed to the white man's culture, most Aborigines experience a compelling desire to remain near white settlements which usually overrides their desire to return to their home country. In a broad sense one can say they were "tricked" into leaving the desert—lured by the promise of abundant food and water along with the excitement of large gatherings of people. But they were not tricked intentionally. Rather, they failed to see the ultimate consequences of settling near the white man, and by the time these consequences became apparent it was too late to go back. At Warburton Betsy and I witnessed the history of this transition as it affected Mitapuyi, Katapi, Minmara, and the other Aborigines we had come to know so well.

A dancer portrays the totemic Magpie.

This dance re-enacts the myth of the totemic Bush-turkey, who during the dreamtime took fire from the other dreamtime people and fled with it. The leader, carrying a string cross (waniki), is the Bush-turkey, and the other dancers are the people pursuing him. The waniki represents the firestick.

Dancers with their bodies painted in the traditional manner re-enact the travels of the dreamtime Carpet-snake; singers, in the background, wear clothes acquired from the Warburton Ranges Mission.

Sacred objects of
a cult-lodge are
displayed to other
lodges while the
novices are being
readied for circum-
cision. A lodge elder is
rubbing a mixture of
red ocher and emu fat
onto an incised
sacred stone.

Ritual blood-letting
before a totemic
Kangaroo-cycle dance.
The tiny sliver of stone
in the "donor's" left
hand was used to open
the arm vein. The
tourniquet on his right
arm controls the flow of
blood.

Carved sacred boards cached inside a rockshelter near Lake Auld. The ceiling is decorated with elaborate paintings.

The "human table" just
before a novice was laid
across it to be circumcised.
(Left) A novice imme-
diately after circumcision,
being congratulated by
his real and classificatory
brothers.

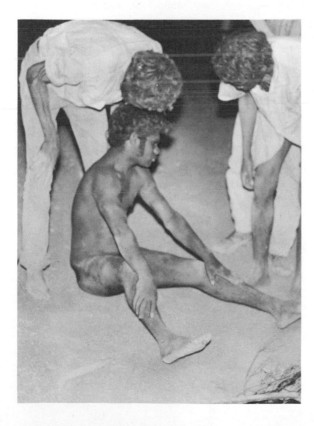

An elderly Ngatatjara man painting designs inside a rockshelter near the Warburton Ranges. The V-shaped designs represent kangaroo or wallaby tracks.

A sacred granite hill near Kunkura waterhole, about 130 miles east of the Warburton Ranges Mission and not far from the place where red ocher was obtained for use in the ritual at Pukara.

In the process of cleaning the sacred waterhole at Pukara, forty-seven stones and pieces of waterlogged wood were dredged out; these are believed to be objects belonging to the totemic Two Water-snakes (Waṇampi Kutjara). The ritual was concluded by painting the waterhole rim with red ocher and by "fingerpainting" elaborate designs on the mud embankment.

The serpentine rock alignment at Lake Moore.

Rockpiles at the sacred dreamtime center at Ngulpiṛ-ngulpiṛ, near the Townsend Range. The rocks are considered to be totemic kampurarpa fruit turned to stone, and increase ceremonies for this plant are performed in the neatly swept spaces around the rockpiles.

Kunmanara venerates an important totemic site (the rock in the foreground) on the track of the dreamtime Opossum, near the Rawlinson Range. His clothes, recently acquired, are the first he has ever owned.

Tjun performs his magical technique for driving away mamu (ghosts).

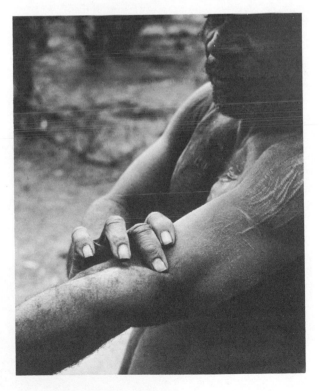

The point of contact for two worlds—Warburton Ranges Mission from the air. (Below) Minmara's camp at the Mission. The area stretching toward the Warburton Ranges in the background has been picked clean by foraging Aborigines.

7

The Dissatisfied

The Department of Health of Western Australia in 1956 investigated conditions at Laverton and the Warburton Ranges. The report issued by the Deputy Commissioner of Public Health stated: ". . . there is some irresistible attraction towards centres of white man's culture that leads more and ever more natives from being aristocrats in the seclusion of their own hunting grounds to graduate through a form of rudimentary education and a system of missions to become unemployables in the squalor of native camps." [1]

Although opportunities for employment have improved somewhat in the last ten years, this statement is essentially as true now as it was then. Indeed, this has been the case wherever white settlements arose in the Australian outback. What is the "irresistible attraction"?

Steel axes and knives, matches, blankets, tea, sugar, flour, rifles, food cans—these are the harbingers of Western civilization. Mundane items like these are the first tangible contact the desert Aborigine has with whites, often long before he sees his first white man. Steel axes, passed along by a chain of relatives, find their way into remote parts of the desert, where they are kept as prized objects. Sometimes Aborigines leave the reserves or missions and return to the bush to rejoin their desert-dwelling relatives, taking with them empty cans, billycans, blankets, and discarded bits of old clothing. Most of the so-called uncontacted groups of Aborigines encountered by government patrols in the Gibson Desert during the last ten years had been exposed indirectly to the white man and his technology in these ways. The simplest artifacts of Western technology provide unparalleled advantages of efficiency and convenience over traditional tools of stone and wood. When Mitapuyi and his family first acquired a steel axhead and a worn metal wood-rasp, they were quick to appreciate the advantages of these over stone tools. While these tools were carefully cached away and guarded when not in use, the desire for more such boons of the white man's bounty grew. When patrols reached this family in 1965, Mitapuyi and the others were easily persuaded to leave the Clutterbuck Hills area and come to the Warburton Ranges Mission.

As the Berndts have observed, the desert Aborigines ". . . simply wanted the novelty of something different—exotic goods, new comforts and luxuries. They did not realize the implications." [2] Objects that first were luxuries or useful appendages to an otherwise fairly successful nomadic life in the desert soon grew to be necessities. It is not easy to persuade Aborigines to resume the laborious traditional practice of making fire by friction when they have become accustomed to matches, and the same is true for other manufactured items. The Mission also had deep bores to provide drinkable water the year round, and a small medical dispensary, both further inducements to the desert Aborigines to live at the Mission. At the time of the national census in June 1966 there were 371 full-blood Aborigines living in the vicinity of the Warburton Ranges Mission, about 60 of whom were desert people who had arrived there within the previous two years. The others had lived in or around the Mission for a longer time, some since the founding of the Mission in 1934. It is likely that many of these Aborigines were enticed to settle there by this same desire for simple objects of European manufacture that had begun to prove so useful. As more and more Aborigines came into the settlement, depopulation of the desert resulted. This accelerated the movement away from the desert, for it meant an increasing shortage of eligible marriage partners. When the Aborigines living on the Mission today speak of the desert where they once lived as being "too lonely," this is the problem to which they are referring.

Gradually but inexorably contact with whites occurred. At first these contacts were only occasional chance encounters with explorers and later with prospectors. With the advent of motor transport, scientific expeditions, such as those directed by the University of South Australia and the South Australian Museum in Adelaide during the 1930s, penetrated deep into the desert, providing additional contacts. The arrival of missionaries and even of some homesteaders quickened the pace, and the climax came in the years following World War II with the construction of the Woomera Rocket Establishment in South Australia. Government patrols equipped with four-wheel-drive vehicles were sent out to reconnoiter the Gibson Desert and adjacent areas in search of Aborigines who, when found, were relocated in settlements like the ones at Warburton and Laverton. This was done for a variety of humanitarian reasons: to keep the Aborigines from being killed or injured by falling rockets, to succor them during severe drought conditions, to bring them the "benefits" of civilization, and so forth. In retrospect, one can only say that contact of some sort was inevitable. The real question now is, should it have come with such a rush? In August 1967 a group of ten nomadic Aborigines was brought into Warburton from the region around Taltiwara, a waterhole about 300 miles northwest of the Mission. Although a few Aborigines are known still to be living in the desert, the resettlement of this group, for all practical purposes, means there are no uncontacted groups left in the desert.

The Warburton "Boom"

Rightly or wrongly, in the last few years the Aborigines at Warburton have been plunged headlong into the white man's world. By Australian or American standards the Warburton Ranges are still extremely remote from civilization, but today there is a graded road and a radio link with the outside world, as well as two graded airstrips and the beginnings of regular air service from Kalgoorlie, about 450 miles away. Geological and mineral surveying parties visit the place frequently, and one firm, the Western Mining Corporation, Ltd., has set up a semipermanent mineral-survey establishment only 3 miles from the Mission. Aborigine men and women sit quietly in front of their lean-tos near the Mission, watching the big trucks roll past and the airplanes land and take off. It is not an exaggeration to say that many of them are contemplating the white man's wealth in material goods and trying to devise ways to partake of it. An altogether new element has come into their lives. For the first time these Aborigines are finding that they cannot satisfy all of their wants in the desert.

The recent "boom" at Warburton had its beginnings in 1961 when an enterprising young Ngatatjara man named Tommy Simms, with the encouragement of the Mission, discovered fairly high-grade deposits of copper ore a few miles away. Tommy's family had traditionally occupied the country in which the Mission is located and was one of the earliest to settle at the Mission, and Tommy had been educated at the Mission school. The period following the discovery was spent in establishing his claim and organizing relatives to help him mine it with hand tools. Before long it was obvious that Tommy and his relatives needed help, and in 1965 the Department of Native Welfare arranged a contract through which a team of four professional miners with machinery belonging to the Western Mining Corporation assisted Tommy in working his claim. The contract provided that the profits of the venture were to be divided into three equal shares among the three parties—Tommy Simms, the miners, and the company. At first the miners tried to find ways to enable Tommy and his relatives to participate in working the claim, but their lack of skills prevented them from doing much useful work. After a while, they spent more and more time simply watching, although this did allow them to become familiar with some of the miners' techniques. The claim was worked for seven months and was closed in May 1966, after 148 tons of high-grade copper ore had been extracted. The total profits at the end were $33,027.36 (Australian), making Tommy's share $11,009.12 ($12,330.21 U.S.).

Tommy Simms' windfall generated considerable excitement, and other Aborigines, mainly relatives of Tommy and other men with at least some Mission-school education, began searching for more copper-ore deposits. Numerous claims were filed, and several shallow hand-excavations were undertaken. Most of the ore found in these was of medium to poor grade, and income barely met expenses (and in some cases did not). The Department of Native Welfare assisted these ventures by advancing money to enable the Aborigine men to purchase food and other necessities from the Mission store so they could work their claims, but, mainly because of the high cost of shipping ore from Warburton to Perth (almost 1000 road-miles away), this proved a losing proposition.

The losses stimulated the department to look for an alternative arrangement, and by September 1966 a contract had been signed with the Western Mining Corporation giving concessions for mineral exploration in several areas near the Warburton Ranges. This contract included terms for training and employing Aborigines in mining jobs as well as payments to Aborigines whose claims were worked. That same month the company began setting up its field station a few miles east of the Mission. Although there were some misunderstandings at the beginning, the overall effect, up to the time my wife and I left in June 1967, had been beneficial for the Aborigines. Many were being trained in useful and well-paid skills, including one young Ngatatjara man who became a technician in the company's field laboratory. These men received a steady income. Theirs was not a windfall like Tommy's, but rather a visible reward for their labor more in line with the expectations of workers in white Australian society.

I suppose nothing epitomized this situation as completely as the sight of Ngatatjara men rising from their campfires and wind-breaks in the morning, going over to the excavations where they operated compressors and other machinery during the day, then returning to camp in the evening to share meat from a kangaroo someone else had killed or to join in a totemic ceremony.

These Aborigine men demonstrated that they were hard workers and intelligent at their job. They acquired skills rapidly and used them well. But the adjustment was not without difficul-ties, some of which remain unresolved. At times, when the labor of working a claim became tedious, some of the men would go off to hunt. They rarely complained that the work was hard, but it was obvious that at times they found the routine boring. Even the desire for wages sometimes could not overcome the greater challenges offered by a good hunt. Sometimes, too, the Ab-origines would leave for a while to attend ceremonies, though, as it happened, these did not conflict seriously with the work sched-ule.

Another problem which some of the white miners encoun-tered was the tendency for a team of Aborigines to sit idly while one of them did all the work. This seemed to happen whenever teams of Aborigines were put to work on their own, with one trained Aborigine in charge. The company, being well-inten-tioned, had wanted to avoid the image of white overseers order-ing natives about, hence they tried to organize all-native work teams. I have mentioned the importance of egalitarianism in traditional Aboriginal life; it extends to the point that a man who orders his peers to do something may be accused of being *wati tjukumunu* (a bossy man). This insult can even apply to elders outside the context of ceremonial occasions. The trained Ab-origine placed in charge of an Aborigine work crew was under-standably reluctant to give orders as were the others to follow them if he did. For him there could be only two ways out of this impasse—give the orders and risk conflict, or do the work himself and try to persuade the others to help. Inevitably the latter solu-tion was the one tried, with the result that conflict was avoided but little work done. In this case the solution to the problem was not difficult. Since the Aborigines regarded the white miners as totally outside their society, they would accept a white foreman without any signs of hostility or feelings of inferiority. Work improved as soon as white foremen were put back in charge.

While all this was happening, Tommy Simms spent his money. Being a traditionally oriented Aborigine, he wanted to be as generous as possible to his kin, but at the same time he wanted the benefits from his new-found fortune to last as long as possible. His solution was to purchase two new vehicles; a 3½-ton Bedford truck and a four-wheel-drive Toyota truck. The Bedford, he declared, was for his relatives to use, and for the most part his brother Harry drove it. Tommy intended the Toyota for his own use and that of his immediate family. Tommy's relatives were happy to take advantage of his bounty and climbed aboard the Bedford in great numbers to go hunting or travel to ceremonies at other, distant reserves. Overloaded, with as many as forty-five men piled on the back at one time and more squeezed into the cab, they made trips to Laverton, Kalgoorlie, Cundeelee, and Musgrave Park. Well do I remember the astonished expression on the face of one elderly white woman on the outskirts of Kalgoorlie as the truck wheeled past. She had been in the back yard of her house stringing up some laundry to dry, when this truck piled high with Aborigines, many of them with their hair long and their bodies painted with red ocher, suddenly arrived and was gone. Kalgoorlie is a fairly large but quiet Australian country town, and sometimes, in an idle moment, I have wondered what she must have thought. No one stopped to explain this apparition to her.

Before long, however, Tommy found that he could not afford to pay for the petrol and maintenance of the Bedford. His repeated pleas that his relatives share the operating costs had little effect. Actually his brother Harry, a more volatile personality than Tommy, triggered most of the arguments over this, but the final outburst came from Tommy. His Toyota had broken down because of a worn-out clutch. While waiting for parts to arrive at Warburton, Tommy tried to get the use of his Bedford to haul firewood to his camp. His request was refused. At this point he and Harry, in a show of fraternal solidarity, marched around the camp shaking their spears and protesting their grievances aloud. Finally they went to the Bedford, which was parked near the Mission, and smashed the windshield and the glass petrol-filter inside the motor. The truck was already in a bad state of repair (to the extent that one of the tires, punctured by mulga stakes, had been stuffed full of spinifex to keep it up), but this intentional damage to the truck in public was extraordinary behavior. Tommy's problem finally achieved a kind of *deus ex machina* solution. The Native Welfare Officer at Warburton proposed that Tommy's relatives rent the vehicle at a fixed rate to cover the cost of petrol and maintenance. This solution was accepted by all and seemed to be working out amiably enough by the time we left the area. By then some of Tommy's relatives were making enough money in wages from mining to be able to afford the "rental." Of course, as in the case of the all-Aborigine mining crews, the problem was resolved, not by any traditional mechanism present in the Aboriginal culture but through intervention by outsiders—that is, whites.

During the months before we left Warburton, other men were starting to acquire cars with their wages. By pooling their resources two or three men could purchase a second-hand car. Most of these cars had short, hard lives, for they were always overloaded with the relatives of the owners and quickly expired on the rough bush tracks around the Mission. Often there were bitter recriminations between co-owners over these breakdowns. Some broke down before they even reached the Mission. On our last trip out in the Land-Rover we counted four of these hulks abandoned along the road between Warburton and Laverton.

For the Aborigines who have shared in it, the Warburton "boom" has been a mixed blessing. They have been able, as in the case of the Bedford truck and the other native-owned vehicles, to acquire manufactured material goods in quantity, but these have not always fitted in smoothly with their traditional and largely kin-based expectations, and arguments and even some fighting have resulted.

Haves and Have-Nots

The Aborigines who have recently arrived at Warburton from the desert have begun to yearn for white goods. But, unlike the Aborigines who have lived at the Mission for a long time, they do not know any English or have any skills which might enable them to work at mining. They live a life apart from the others and, so far, have been unable to participate directly in the "boom."

About the only employment open to the desert people is weapon-making for tourists. This is handled through the Native Welfare Officer, who receives orders for boomerangs, spearthrowers, clubs, and shields from Perth and gets various Aborigines to carve them. The Aborigines are paid a fixed price for each artifact, but the market fluctuates and is too small to mean very much. At Warburton and Laverton I have also seen acculturated Aborigines move in as middlemen in these situations, acting as go-betweens for the desert people and the whitefella and pocketing most of the payment in the process. Incidentally, the boomerang is the favorite souvenir of tourists to Australia and the outback. Since returning boomerangs were not traditionally made or used by the Ngatatjara, the Department of Native Welfare had to devise a boomerang template for the Aborigines to copy. The visitor to Warburton today will see an abundance of these virtually mass-produced boomerangs made for tourist consumption.

The other Aborigines call the desert people the "kayili [northern] mob," or, when they want to be unkind, the "lizard eaters." It is traditional desert etiquette that visitors settle on the side of the camp which is in the direction from which they came. Since all these desert people come from such places as Lake Macdonald, Taltiwara, Tika-tika, and the Clutterbuck Hills—that is, from the area north of the Warburton Ranges—they live on the northern edge of the camp. When relations are good they tend to camp close to the others, but more often feelings are strained between the factions and there may be as much as 800 to 1000 feet of intervening ground between the respective camps. Even in the remote Gibson Desert it is possible to find a sort of miniature ghetto.

As I discovered while collecting genealogies during late 1966, the physical distance between the camps of the two factions is matched by an equally wide gulf of social distance.[3] Although Betsy and I recorded ninety-four marriages, within the previous two years only one had occurred between a desert family and a family of Aborigines long established at the Mission. This marriage was not widely approved by the latter faction. Although there were a few distant kinship ties between the two families, there were no other connections which would enable the desert family to share the relative affluence of the others.

Coupled with this lack of kinship ties I also found instances of overt hostility between Aborigines established at the Mission and the newcomers. The "kayili mob" were often accused of being troublemakers with quick tempers. They also had a reputation as powerful sorcerers. Because of their lack of kinship relations to the others, the desert people were regarded by some of the other Aborigines as fair game to be exploited and even abused, as in the instance described earlier when a Warburton man took Katapi's thirteen-year-old daughter Tanara into the bush with him.

Because they are badly outnumbered, the newcomers cannot risk a test of strength in quarrels between themselves and the others. They have what amounts to two alternatives open to them: they can flee back into the desert or they can remain at Warburton, continuing to suffer indignities, and find ways to intermarry with the Aborigines who have lived there longer. During 1966–67 both alternatives were being tried. The first was tried by two groups: one family which asked to be taken back to the Taltiwara region and Mitapuyi and his relatives who returned on their own to the Clutterbuck Hills area. At best this solution is only temporary, since inevitably the children will want to marry and they can now do so only by moving to a reserve or mission. Most of the desert people realize that times have changed, and however unpleasant it may be at first, they must stay at the Mission and try to make the best of it for themselves and their children.

Having made this choice, they have begun taking steps to integrate themselves with the others. The initiative for this integration has come entirely from the desert people and has involved a basic restructuring of their social organization to make it compatible with that of the Aborigines at the Mission. The first step has been to try to make intermarriage possible between the two factions.

In Chapter 5 I described the system of six intermarrying sections which prevails among the Aborigines of the Warburton

Ranges area. This serves, among other things, to regulate marriages among all the people who have lived at Warburton for a long time, and it also operates among the Aborigines living at Laverton and Mount Margaret (a mission about twenty miles from Laverton). The desert people from the north, however, are accustomed to a system which, though similar in principle and function to the six-section arrangement, is made up of eight intermarrying categories (called subsections by anthropologists).

SUBSECTIONS		SECTIONS	DIVISIONS
Tjakamara × Nyapaltjari	= $\dfrac{\text{Tjupurula}}{\text{Nyapurula}}$	Panaka/Yiparka	"sun"
Tjampitjin × Nyapangati	= $\dfrac{\text{Tjangala}}{\text{Nyangala}}$		
Tjapaltjari × Nyakamara	= $\dfrac{\text{Tjungurayi}}{\text{Nyungurayi}}$	Tjaruru	
Tjapangati × Nyampitjin	= $\dfrac{\text{Tjapanyangka}}{\text{Nyapanyangka}}$		
Tjangala × Nyungurayi	= $\dfrac{\text{Tjampitjin}}{\text{Nyampitjin}}$	Karimara/Milangka	"shade"
Tjupurula × Nyapanyangka	= $\dfrac{\text{Tjakamara}}{\text{Nyakamara}}$		
Tjungurayi × Nyangala	= $\dfrac{\text{Tjapaltjari}}{\text{Nyapaltjari}}$	Purungu	
Tjapanyangka × Nyapurula	= $\dfrac{\text{Tjapangati}}{\text{Nyapangati}}$		

×	marriage	Tj-	male prefix
=	offspring	Ny-	female prefix

Each of these has both a male and a female prefix, giving a total of sixteen names. This subsection system bears a close resemblance to that of the Walbiri tribe of Northern Territory described by Meggitt.[4] Almost none of the Aborigines who have lived at the Mission a long time know the names of all the desert people's subsections or show any interest in learning them— further evidence of the disdain with which they regard the newcomers.

As a prerequisite to intermarriage between the two factions, these different systems must be equated. The desert people have worked out a series of equivalents between their eight-subsection system and the six-section system at Warburton. The table on page 175 summarizes the way this has been accomplished.

The best way to understand how this system of equivalents operates is to test it against the six-section system diagrammed in Chapter 5. For example, if you, the reader, are a Tjakamara man, you are, according to this set of equivalents, the same as a Karimara/Milangka man among the missionized "six-section" people. You must marry a Nyapaltjari woman, who, by these same rules, is the same as a Puṛungu, and your resulting offspring are Tjupurula/Nyapurula (that is, equivalent to Panaka/Yiparka). This is a legal or "right" marriage for both the desert people, with their subsections, and the mission people, with their sections.

The Berndts have correctly classified the Warburton Ranges as an area of "rapprochement" between section and subsection systems.[5] The rapprochement in this case has been initiated entirely by the recently arrived desert Aborigines to prepare the way for intermarriage with the established group at Warburton. Of course they are motivated to do this by their basic desire to see their children marry and raise offspring. However, they also see marriage as a means to further ends, namely, setting up kinship ties with the other faction which will allow them to share in the material wealth of the white man and ensure immunity from the indignities to which they are presently subjected. Their effort to equate the two systems has been a fully conscious one. I have been present when there were discussions and even arguments about how to equate the various sections and subsections. One byproduct of this effort has been a shrewd analysis of the six-section system in which they correctly ascertained the relative unimportance of two of the sections—Milangka and Yiparka. These two they have lumped together with Panaka and Karimara, respectively, to provide a true picture of the way they operate as "extra" or redundant sections in what is really a four-section system. Moreover, all the equivalents thus arrived at also fit within the framework of the "sun" and "shade" divisions, with their alternating generations.

As a short-term solution to the desert people's problem as "have-nots" in the Warburton community this effort will probably succeed. But they also have begun to appreciate the value of the education their children are receiving in the government-run school [6] at Warburton as a long-term solution to their problem. In part their enthusiasm for their children's education stems from the ration of food each child receives in school, but I also know that these people, even though they have been in from the desert only a short time, are aware that the children are gaining skills which will enable them to work at jobs in the same way as the other educated Aborigines.

Among the genealogies we collected I found one case of a Rawlinson Range man belonging to the Tjupurula subsection (that is, equivalent to Panaka/Yiparka) who married a Tjaruru woman before he came to live at any reserve or mission. There is no way of knowing exactly how long ago this marriage took place, but it does suggest that a system of equating sections and subsections must have been taking shape even before some of these people left the desert. This impression is reinforced by the observations of Dr. Henry K. Fry, an Australian anthropologist from Adelaide University, who observed some equivalents between section and subsection systems in use among previously uncontacted desert Aborigines around Mount Liebig in Northern Territory.[7] What probably happened was that adjustments were made in individual cases and these became more common as depopulation of the desert increased and people had to look farther afield for marriage partners. As more and more families were taken out of the desert and brought together at the Mission, it became necessary to make more such adjustments, and through arguments and discussions these individual adjustments became regularized into the system now in use. Today the desert people are able to switch easily from one system to the other in their conversation whenever the situation demands it. This behavior caused me some confusion at first. While I was living in the desert with Mitapuyi's and Walanya's families, I had inquired about their subsection affiliations. Initially they answered me with terms used in the six-section system, mainly out of courtesy to me, since at that time they associated Betsy and me with the other people at the Warburton Ranges—after all, we did call ourselves Panaka and Tjaruru. I had to make a special request that they forget this courtesy and speak in terms of their own subsection usage before I found out what I wanted to know.

The Warburton Scene Today

The first glimpse a visitor today has of the Aborigines at Warburton is not encouraging. He sees between 400 and 500 full-blood Aborigines[8] in cast-off clothing, living in brush windbreaks and lean-tos constructed from odd sheets of scrap metal, old mattresses and tarpaulins, and other items scrounged from the Missions. Bits of paper and empty food tins litter the ground. He observes a few Aborigines at work in the Mission area—chopping firewood, carving boomerangs, making sun-dried bricks, or doing laundry for the whites. If he travels through the country a few miles beyond the Mission he will see some more men working at mining, and he will probably encounter a few men out hunting and some women foraging for seeds and other edibles. Most of the children are in school during the day. But many Aborigines can be found sitting either in camp or, on days when rations are handed out,[9] in the Mission area.

Over the years, Aborigines have removed much of the natural vegetation around the Mission in their incessant search for food and firewood. Digging for roots containing grubs has killed trees, and fires have thinned the natural cover in many places. The broad expanse of the airfield and numerous vehicle tracks have carried this process even further, so when the wind blows hard the whole area is blanketed by clouds of choking red dust. From thirty miles away one can see an immense column of dust towering thousands of feet into the air over the Warburton Mission during one of these windstorms. This only adds to the generally miserable look of the place.

The Warburton Mission today is overrun with dogs. Mainly these are dingoes or part-dingoes that have interbred with dogs owned by whites. The Aborigines treat puppies with real affection. They pet them (a favorite form of petting is to fondle the dogs' genitals), and even at the Mission or on reserves a woman suckling a puppy is still a common sight. There is no restraint on dogs' breeding, and the Mission staff and Native Welfare authorities have done nothing to control their numbers. Except for one or two which a man or woman regards as favorites, the dogs are not fed or cared for in any way. They scavenge singly or in packs in and around the camp and find barely enough food to keep them alive. They look emaciated, and, as the Native Welfare Officer put it one day, "They have just enough energy left to breed."

To the field worker, this overabundance of dogs constitutes a minor but nevertheless constant source of annoyance. Whenever we left our tent for even a short time, the dogs entered and ransacked it, devouring magazines, tubes of condensed milk, string, typing paper, and anything else not locked inside steel trunks. In one instance they even bit open a can of corned beef and licked out most of the contents. After repeated incursions of this kind we gave up living in the tent and moved to a small hut which the missionaries allowed us to use whenever we stayed at the Mission. Sometimes, I might add, the Aborigines get fed up with the dogs, too. During one very hot day the whole camp was roused by the screams and curses of an old woman who had been pestered by the dogs all afternoon. Finally she could stand it no longer, and taking a crowbar she had been using as a digging-stick she flailed at all the dogs around her. For a few minutes there was utter pandemonium—then silence. She had killed five dogs and maimed at least a half-dozen more.

One morning I drove the Land-Rover into the kayili camp on my way to purchase a hair-string belt that Nyurapaya had made. This was before Mitapuyi and the others had returned to the desert, but they knew Betsy and me well enough by then to have fitted us into their kinship and subsection systems. The Land-Rover's brakes had been giving trouble for some time, so I approached the camp slowly, at perhaps twenty miles per hour. As I did, a pack of well over 100 dogs rushed out from camp toward the vehicle. I could not dodge them without risk of running into one of the people in camp, so I kept the truck straight as I wrestled it to a stop. The press of dogs from behind forced the leaders of the pack right under my wheels, killing a couple outright and injuring several others. The owner of one of the dogs, an elderly Ngatatjara man named Mungulu, rushed over from his camp on the other side of the creekbed and demanded compensation. Although in a way he was entitled to it, I knew he had never cared for the dog and was using its death as a convenient way to worm some tobacco out of me. I expressed my regrets but refused to pay him, saying he should have tied up the dog if he wanted to keep it from being run over. Mungulu was angry and so was I, and we were both being a little pig-headed. I walked away to Mitapuyi's camp while Mungulu went off by himself, muttering.

Later, after I paid Nyurapaya with some tobacco, she divided it into shares which she passed around to her relatives, including Mitapuyi. As I was leaving I noticed Mitapuyi taking his share over to Mungulu's camp. As my classificatory uncle (Mitapuyi belongs to the Tjapaltjari subsection and hence is equivalent to Puṟungu; this means that I, as a Panaka man, addressed him as "kamuṟu [mother's brother]"), he felt responsible for me. He did not really approve of my conduct but preferred at that time not to tell me so directly, though he did later. Rather than tell me to compensate Mungulu for the loss of his dog, he preferred to settle the matter himself by acting on my behalf, thus smoothing relations with Mungulu without being bossy toward me. His avuncular behavior toward me, I realized later, was carried out with remarkable tact and saved me from possible future conflict. Without the sympathetic support of people like Mitapuyi my field work could easily have come to grief over some such relatively trivial issue as dogs.

Although tobacco, as I have mentioned, grows wild in parts of the desert, hardly any grows near the Mission. Out of religious conviction the missionaries refuse to supply any to the Aborigines, and only recently has the Native Welfare Officer taken steps to get tobacco which the men earning wages at mining can buy. Throughout our stay at Warburton, I exchanged tobacco (in the form of plugs and sometimes cigarettes) for goods, information, and favors such as being allowed to observe a ceremony or being taught a song. I was, in fact, the Aborigines' chief source of supply and soon became known as *mingkultjara* (he who has tobacco).

Traditionally all tobacco is chewed into a ball, then mixed with some ash formed from burning green Acacia leaves, and chewed again. At ceremonies and other gatherings a man will usually pass his premasticated ball of tobacco to a relative as part of the sharing normally expected among kin. Sometimes this ball of tobacco is stored behind an ear or under the lip between chewings. One sign of changing times at Warburton is the rising popularity of cigarette smoking among the young men. (The older men still prefer to tear open a cigarette and chew the tobacco.) Because the young men like to wear cowboy hats, which interfere with the behind-the-ear technique of storing tobacco, they keep the premasticated balls of tobacco in bunches of a half-dozen or so inside cigarette-paper cans. Now, when they sit down for ceremonies or to sing sacred songs, it is considered the height of fashion to pass these circular cans around like a plate of hors d'oeuvres at a cocktail party; each relative chooses the morsel he wants and pops it into his mouth.

Though the camps of the nomadic desert Aborigines were not particularly hygienic, at Warburton the conditions of general filth are multiplied by the fact that so many people have been drawn to this single place where they remain together most of the time. Sometimes the camp as a whole is moved to another spot, say from the east to the north side of the Mission, but always in the same general area within about a half-mile radius. When we left in 1967 the Department of Native Welfare was drawing up plans for setting up housing for Aborigines near the Mission, but no work had started on the project.

Given these living conditions, it is not surprising that one of the first things that happens to desert Aborigines when they arrive at the Mission is measles, sometimes in conjunction with other ailments such as gastroenteritis and colds. These illnesses, relatively mild when contracted by Europeans, can have a devastating effect on the Aborigines, who in most cases have almost no natural immunity to them. The Mission requires the Aborigines living there to wear clothing, another factor which fosters disease. The recently arrived Aborigines, who of course know nothing about washing their clothes, allow them to become caked with dirt through constant wear in camp, and, to make matters worse, they stand around in wet clothing after rains. When epidemics occur, the two nursing sisters at the Mission do what they can, sometimes enlisting the help of the Royal Flying Doctor Service[10] by radio. If conditions are serious enough, the doctor is flown up from Kalgoorlie, and a critically ill patient (if he will allow himself to be flown in an airplane) can be airlifted to the hospital there.

One morning a young Ngatatjara man recently arrived from the desert came to me in a state of obvious excitement. He explained that he and his relatives had gone hunting in rugged country to the north of the Warburton Ranges, where all the others had become desperately sick. For some reason he was unaffected and had walked in on his own. He pleaded with me to drive out in the Land-Rover and get them. As luck would have it, ours was the only four-wheel-drive vehicle then in running condition at the Mission. I agreed to help, and we filled the tanks and set off immediately. The trip was about thirty miles through thick mulga and several narrow gullies. When we finally arrived, the sight which awaited us could not have been more ominous. Most of the people lay on the ground in various places near their windbreaks. Except for a couple of children who were walking around, nobody moved. After a short wait while my guide wailed to express sympathy for the others we started carrying people to the Land-Rover. A few could walk, but most had to be helped or carried and piled like cordwood in the back. In all I took seventeen people (not counting myself) back to the Mission in the Land-Rover that day. It was a miserable trip for my passengers, for the track was just as rough going back, and the day had grown hot. There were some groans from the back whenever we hit a bad bump, but on the whole they suffered in silence—which made me worry about them even more. At last we reached the Mission, and a call was put through on the radio for the Flying Doctor.

These people had contracted measles while they were camping at the Mission. They had received treatment from the nurses and responded well—so well, in fact, that they thought they were cured and so set off for the bush. There they had a relapse. Along with measles, several of the children had gastroenteritis. Under the circumstances there might have been a number of fatalities, but only one child died. Before I arrived, the mother, sick herself, had set off on her own with the child to try to get back to the Mission. She took a route across stony ground, so there was no hope of following her tracks. When she reached the Mission the next day she was carrying the dead child. All the others had the benefit of the heroic efforts of the nurses, and of the Flying Doctor, who flew up every day that week, and eventually they recovered.

Aside from a few scraps of clothing that get passed along into the desert by relatives, the Aborigines receive their first clothes from a patrol or when they arrive at the Mission. These they willingly accept, though sometimes they have to struggle mightily to get them on and off. At first they wear the clothes mainly out of courtesy toward the whites, for in the desert climate clothing is unnecessary except perhaps on cold nights. In time, however, clothing, no matter how ragged, becomes a sort of prestige item, like other manufactured goods acquired from the white man. It is not modesty or necessity that persuades the Aborigines to wear clothes on the Mission, but the desire to avoid offending the whites and to obtain the status that comes from possessing a pair of trousers or an old jacket. In the desert they prefer not to wear the clothing, at least in hot weather. As often as not, when a family has been back in the desert for a while, the people wrap their clothing in a bundle and cache this in a tree. If a white person happens along, the bundles are opened and the clothes put back on, mainly because the Aborigines think that all whites are sensitive in this matter. Once I was traveling in the lead vehicle of a desert patrol when we paid a visit to Tika-tika. I knew that Nyurapaya, Katapi, and Tjanangu would be camped there, along with little Ngampakatju. We arrived during the heat of midday, and, because I knew the way in to the camp, we approached swiftly. The women had been asleep, so they were not aware of our presence until we were fairly close. It was a warm day, and they had no clothes on. When they heard our vehicles coming they raced around to collect the clothing they had with them, and when we arrived they were still struggling to get everything on.

Later, when these families came to know my wife and me better, they were much less concerned about wearing clothes in our presence when we were all in the desert. On the Mission, however, the young men and women, mainly those who have been to school, are becoming more conscious of clothes. The teen-age girls try to get colorful dresses, while the young men sport rakish cowboy hats and boots. I recall one young desert Aborigine who was teased mercilessly by the more missionized girls about his appearance. One day he appeared with the traditional mud-curls in his hair gone. He had his hair cut short and wore a cowboy hat, boots, and trousers held up by a thick belt with an enormous shiny buckle. He had had enough teasing, he said, and this seemed to him the best way to get the girls to notice him. He had worked for the Mission to earn money to buy these garments, and the sudden transformation in his appearance was typical of what is happening these days at Warburton.

While some of the white man's fashions are accepted fairly readily, other practices change slowly or not at all. Out of the 94 marriages we recorded at Warburton in late 1966, 13 were polygynous. Or, to put it differently, 94 men were married to 111 women, making an average of 1.2 wives per husband.

WIVES PER MARRIED MAN

NUMBER OF WIVES	1	2	3	4	5
FREQUENCY	81	11	1	0	1

This is a slightly lower incidence of polygyny than that recorded by Meggitt for a comparable sample of Walbiri marriages,[11] but it indicates, nevertheless, that polygyny has remained popular among Aborigines at Warburton even after over thirty years of efforts by missionaries to discourage it.

Nor has the Aboriginal attitude toward the sacred life changed drastically as a result of mission influence. Many Aborigines whom the Mission regards as converts (mostly younger men and women) are quite sincere in their acceptance of Christianity but regard it as an addition to their totemic beliefs. Paul Porter, our much-esteemed guide, attended the native-language Christian service at the Mission on Sunday morning and later the same day might be seen participating in totemic ceremonies in the bush. Once I asked him if he saw anything contradictory in his behavior, and he said no. As he and other men put it: "*Tji:tjaku ṯuḻku maḻu yiwara pinpa* [Jesus' sacred law is just like the totemic Kangaroo's track]." That is, these converts regarded Jesus as another totemic being worthy of veneration. They did not lack religious sincerity, only monotheism.

Some of the recent changes at Warburton are ominous in character. Perhaps most serious of all is theft. Stealing is unheard of among Aborigines living in the bush, where material possessions are limited to the few things one can carry or put away in a cache and where one can always satisfy the need for a spear, club, or other item by asking the appropriate relative for one. Once settled at the Mission, however, Aborigines could acquire and accumulate material possessions to a degree never before possible. Theft was hardly known at Warburton until the year we arrived there. Shortly before I paid my first visit to the Mission, the miners who had assisted Tommy Simms in working his claim discovered that their house had been broken into and their tobacco stolen. Later, the boys who had committed the crime returned the loot and apologized, and the problem seemed to have taken care of itself. But a few months later large amounts of gasoline were siphoned off during the night from drums stored near the Mission store. Since there were several native-owned cars running at the time, it was never determined exactly who stole the gasoline, but from then on the supplies were kept in a locked storehouse. Not long after that some young men broke into the store and were seen by one of the missionaries as they ran off with armloads of goods. At this point a policeman was called in from Leonora, over 450 miles away, to apprehend the men and put a stop to the stealing. The men could have fled into the bush but chose instead to give themselves up and ultimately received light sentences in the local jail at Leonora.

I might add that a jail sentence carries little or no stigma among the Aborigines, who generally regard it as a good way of leaving the outback for a while and seeing the world (rather like the "grand tour" taken by a novice before his circumcision). One acculturated Aborigine we talked to at Laverton recalled with pride that he had seen Perth as a young man during his stay at the Fremantle Prison. This had been a novel experience which he said he had enjoyed. He had been housed and fed free of charge and could sit around all day learning sacred songs from the other Aborigine inmates. It seemed to him a queer sort of punishment, but really no more puzzling than a lot of things the whitefella did.

Another recent development at Warburton is an increase in "begging." At the moment this is less of a problem there than at many other towns such as Laverton and Leonora, where Aborigines importune travelers and visitors on the streets for tobacco and at times for money and food. Often, too, they will attempt to sell poorly made boomerangs and other artifacts to visitors this way. Raggedly dressed Aborigines attempting to beg or sell on street corners are even seen in larger towns like Alice Springs and Kalgoorlie. Often these are the only Aborigines a tourist encounters, and this behavior inevitably creates a bad impression.

A strange kind of logic prevails in such situations. An Aborigine will often address a whitefella as *kuṭa* (elder brother) or *katja* (son, nephew) in the hope that the white man will respond appropriately by sharing some tobacco or other desired commodity with him. The whitefella does not know what the Aborigine is talking about, but, out of the goodness of his heart or perhaps in exchange for taking a few snapshots, he may give the Aborigine some cigarettes. The two parties view the transaction with opposite expectations. At this point the white man thinks that he has discharged any obligation he may have or at least has forestalled any further claims. The Aborigine, however, sees the gift as an affirmation of some sort of kin-bond, and before long he returns, often with several of his relatives, to ask for more. In his view, the fact that the white man gave him something the first time entitled him to ask again, both for himself and his relatives. The Aborigine may persist in his "begging" until the white man becomes thoroughly fed up and with much grimacing and hand-gesturing orders the native away. Such encounters can cause hurt feelings and aroused tempers on both sides.

Another distressing recent development is the tendency for young men to sell sacred artifacts, particularly carved boards and sacred stones, to visitors passing through Warburton. This practice has already reached serious proportions at Laverton and is beginning to at Warburton. In many cases the sacred objects have been stolen in the bush from caches belonging to totemic lodges. The lodge elders are not aware of what has happened until too late. Under traditional circumstances this kind of stealing not only is as unthinkable as any other kind, but has the added element of sacrilege. The Department of Native Welfare is presently taking steps to construct storage sheds at Laverton and Warburton where the lodge elders may keep sacred artifacts under lock and key. This should reduce the thefts somewhat and also eliminate the danger of whites accidentally finding sacred caches in their travels through the bush and looting them. However, the mere presence of this type of theft by Aborigines indicates that respect for the sacred life is gradually being overcome, not by missionaries, but by an insatiable desire for the white man's material goods.

Perhaps the best way to sum up the present situation at Warburton is to state that the Aborigines are at present a dependent population, basing their existence increasingly on welfare administered by the government and the Mission. Like other dependent populations, they have little or nothing to sell to the Western market economy—in this case, only a few boomerangs and their labor. The present mineral boom offers the hope of an escape from this dependent status, but only if enough copper and other valuable minerals are discovered to make full-scale mining profitable and if the present policy of training and hiring Aborigines is maintained. Admittedly it is too late for many Aborigines in other parts of Australia, where loss of cultural traditions and dependence on welfare aid have progressed much further. But at Warburton there is still at least a chance that the Aborigines may be able to preserve the dignity of their traditions under a system of profitable employment.

Image in the Mirror

The scene at the Warburton Ranges Mission today shows Aborigines starting to behave the way we do in Western society. Their lives are a kind of mirror in which our way of life is reflected, but the image we see is grotesque. Much of the distortion comes from adherence to traditions which lose their meaning once these people leave the desert. Why continue to hold increase ceremonies for natural species when your "dreaming" site is too far away to visit and your food supply mostly "whitefella tucker" anyway? Sometimes the chance juxtaposition of elements from the two different worlds creates comical and even bizarre effects. How proud old Tjupurula was of the cast-off coat he was given from the Mission box. Regal dark blue with brass buttons, gold shoulderboards, and three gold stripes on each sleeve, this lordly piece of men's wear was probably worn only on formal occasions by the captain of some now-forgotten ship. Tjupurula, however, wore it constantly in camp and in the bush, even when he had nothing else on.

Most significantly, however, the Aborigines show a completely undisguised avarice for the white man's material goods. This avarice touches every Aborigine family at Warburton, whether they have lived there twenty years or only six months. Some Aborigines desire things they had never even heard of six months or a year earlier. No matter how much they have amassed and given to relatives, they still desire more. My last glimpse of Tommy Simms before we left Warburton was as he headed off to the Townshend Range in his battered Toyota to look for more copper ore. While the desert people are devising ways to intermarry with more prosperous Aborigines who settled at the Mission long ago, the latter are also devising schemes for acquiring more money and goods. Some are working at jobs for the mining company or the Mission; others are looking for a more prosperous relative to "share" with (a one-sided kind of sharing, more akin to sponging); a few are leaving the Mission to look for jobs on sheep stations, and others are "begging" from the whitefella or stealing.

The Aborigines' consuming desire for material goods is expressed without any of the niceties of European convention. The "begging" I have referred to is in most cases not a matter of asking politely for something but of demanding it. The arrangements for intermarriage between the two factions are made in a no-nonsense, businesslike atmosphere, with marriage viewed as a transaction and an alliance between two blocs of kin rather than in any romantic or passionate sense. This behavior is in keeping with traditional Aboriginal attitudes but the result is that the white visitor sees the Aborigines' dissatisfaction in a blatant, unvarnished form. The ultimate expression of this dissatisfaction is the stealing, which letters from friends at Warburton indicate has increased even more since we left. This is neither traditional nor polite behavior; it expresses the frustrations felt by people who desire more than they can acquire by other means.

Epilogue

When Betsy and I returned to the United States in July 1967, we encountered the hurly-burly of American life with a heightened awareness of its essential nature. For a short time we had left one world and stepped into another. Our world—that is, America and Western society generally—is filled with clashing demands from an overwhelming number of groups, all of which had one thing in common—dissatisfaction. Strident protests of dissatisfaction about the war in Vietnam filled the air, no less vehement on one side of the issue than on the other. More to the point, Negro dissatisfaction had reached a point where pressure by violence and looting had become commonplace. Private dissatisfactions over wages, working conditions, and other matters manifested themselves in a succession of strikes, and college students, no less than workers, showed their discontent by staging sit-ins and student strikes.

The world that we glimpsed briefly in the desert was different. The nomadic Aborigines could derive personal satisfaction both from their ability to cope with the practical problems of living in the desert and in their sacred lives, through kin ties linking them to the land and its natural species. A man could measure his own worth directly by his success as a provider for his kin and his progress through the stages of cult totemism. Until the sticky tentacles of Western society first reached the Aborigine in the form of a steel ax and a secondhand description of the white man's ways, his main desire was to see his life and that of his children arranged the same way that his ancestors' lives had been.

Our sojourn at the Warburton Ranges and in the Gibson Desert in 1966–67 placed us amid a state of flux. I was able almost simultaneously to satisfy my curiosity about the nature of a traditional hunting and foraging way of life in the desert and to observe the essential changes being brought about by white contact. To be sure, my evaluation of the traditional nomadic life of the Aborigines is subjective in the sense that it is based on close personal experiences rather than on data which can be tested and measured objectively. Other fully competent scientists may disagree with my estimate of Aboriginal life, but I did not have any built-in sympathies for the Aborigines before we arrived in the desert. My appreciation of them arose from my experiences with them, not from any romantic ideal or image of the "noble savage"—an attitude which, indeed, anthropologists nowadays are rigorously trained to avoid.

In looking back I also realized that my experience involved a sharp irony which is true, in varying degrees, of the field experiences of other anthropologists. The technology and specialization which have enabled Western society to invade remote parts of the world and change the lives of the native inhabitants have also produced anthropologists and enabled them to learn about these peoples and their traditions. As long as the Gibson Desert Aborigines remained isolated, they remained unknown. When their isolation was broken and they became known, they began to change with phenomenal speed.

At the Warburton Ranges Mission, right before our eyes, my wife and I had seen the transformation caused by closer contact with whites, as desert families settled there. From tiny beginnings their dissatisfaction with their lot has grown rapidly to Western proportions, accelerated, no doubt, by the recent boom in mining. The Aborigines who had lived there longer were even more blatant in expressing their dissatisfactions. The rise of petty thievery at Warburton and the recent looting by Negroes and others in American cities, though a hemisphere apart, are both manifestations of the same deep discontent and dissatisfaction which are essentially characteristic of Western civilization.

The story of the Ngatatjara Aborigines at Warburton shows that *dissatisfaction with things as they are is not an essential attribute of human nature.* For the desert people it is a characteristic acquired from their contact with Western society. While I do not advocate isolating the Australian Aborigines or other people like them into perpetual "zoos" or preserves away from white influences, I must admit to feeling that mankind as a whole may be suffering an irretrievable loss with the passing of their societies. We will never again know firsthand how it felt to lead the sort of foraging and hunting life that man has lived throughout most of his past.

Today the Gibson Desert is the loneliest place on earth, lonelier even than the wastes of Antarctica. What can be lonelier than a place where people have lived their lives and then left forever? Now the same sense of melancholy that blankets an ancient ruined city covers the Australian desert, where the sandhills lie silent in the blazing sun and the gleeful shouts of children chasing a lizard through the spinifex are heard no longer.

Notes

CHAPTER 1: A DAY WITH THE DESERT PEOPLE

1. Walanya is the only member of this group to have lived for very long at the Warburton Ranges Mission. His name is the native rendering of Wallace (the suffix -*nya* denotes a proper name; in all other cases I have simplified by omitting the suffix). Walanya is Nyurapaya's elder brother, whom Mitapuyi addresses as *makunta*. But the real "glue" which keeps these two families together is the close affection which Nyurapaya and Katapi have for each other. They are inseparable and camp and forage together whenever they can.
2. David W. Carnegie, *Spinifex and Sand* (New York: M. F. Mansfield and Co., 1898), 234, and Donald F. Thomson, "A Bark Sandal from the Desert of Central Western Australia," *Man*, LX, Article No. 228 (1960), 177–79. For a general discussion of the subject see D. Sutherland Davidson, "Footwear of the Australian Aborigines: Environmental vs. Cultural Determination," *Southwestern Journal of Anthropology*, III, No. 2 (1947), 114–23.
3. Douglas Lockwood, *The Lizard Eaters* (Melbourne: Cassel, Ltd., 1964).
4. Richard A. Gould, "Notes on Hunting, Butchering, and Sharing of Game Among the Ngatatjara and Their Neighbors in the West Australian Desert," *Kroeber Anthropological Society Papers*, No. 36 (1967), 41–66.
5. Richard A. Gould, "Chipping Stones in the Outback," *Natural History*, LXXVII, No. 2 (1968), 42–49; also Donald F. Thomson, "Some Wood and Stone Implements of the Bindibu Tribe of Central Western Australia," *Proceedings of the Prehistoric Society for 1964*, XXX, No. 17 (1964), 400–22, and Norman B. Tindale, "Stone Implement Making among the Nakako, Ngadadjara and Pitjand-

jara of the Great Western Desert," *Records of the South Australian Museum,* XV, No. 1 (1965), 131–64.

CHAPTER 2: THE GIBSON DESERT AND ITS EARLY
EXPLORERS

1. Ernest Giles, *Australia Twice Traversed* (London: Sampson Low, Marston, Searle and Rivington, Ltd., 1889), I, 191.
2. *Ibid.,* 92.
3. D. J. Mulvaney, "The Prehistory of the Australian Aborigine," *Scientific American,* Vol. 214, No. 3 (1966), 89.
4. Figures cited in T. G. H. Strehlow, "Culture, Social Structure, and Environment in Aboriginal Central Australia," in *Aboriginal Man in Australia,* R. M. and C. H. Berndt, eds. (Sydney: Angus and Robertson, Ltd., 1965), 122.
5. Figures cited in Mervyn J. Meggitt, *Desert People* (Sydney: Angus and Robertson, Ltd., 1962), 1.
6. Giles, *op. cit.,* 292.
7. This early phase of Australian desert exploration is described in several different summaries. Two of the best are: Kathleen Fitzpatrick, *Australian Explorers* (London: Oxford University Press, 1958), and Geoffrey Rawson, *Desert Journeys* (London: Jonathan Cape, Ltd., 1948).
8. Quoted in Fitzpatrick, *op. cit.,* 418.
9. *Ibid.,* 432.
10. Giles, *op. cit.,* II, 47.
11. *Ibid.,* 41.
12. *Ibid.,* 321.
13. Helms kept a diary of anthropological observations during the Elder Exploring Expedition of 1891. These were published, along with some general observations on Australian Aborigines, in a scientific report which, though sketchy, gives the first detailed picture of uncontacted Aborigines living in the Everard to the Barrow Ranges (to a point about 50 miles east of the Warburtons) and the Victoria Desert to the Fraser Range (near the present town of Norseman, Western Australia). Richard Helms, "Anthropology of the Elder Exploring Expedition," *Transactions of the Royal Society of South Australia,* XVI (1896), 237–332.
14. Giles, *op. cit.,* I, 298.
15. *Ibid.,* 315.

CHAPTER 3: WHO ARE THE DESERT ABORIGINES?

1. N. W. Thomas, *Natives of Australia* (London: Archibald Constable and Company, Ltd., 1906), 18.
2. George F. Angas, *Savage Life and Scenes in Australia and New Zealand* (London: Smith, Elder, and Company, Ltd., 1847), I, 82.
3. W. Baldwin Spencer and F. J. Gillen, *The Native Tribes of Central Australia* (London: Macmillan and Company, Ltd., 1899).
4. See W. J. Sollas, *Ancient Hunters and Their Modern Representatives* (London: Macmillan and Company, Ltd., 1925), 258–59.
5. Herbert M. Hale and Norman B. Tindale, "Notes on Some Human Remains in the Lower Murray Valley, South Australia," *Records of the South Australian Museum*, IV (1930), 145–218.
6. Carmel White, Plateau and Plain. Unpublished Ph.D. dissertation, Department of Anthropology, Australian National University, Canberra, 1968.
7. Mulvaney, *op. cit.*, 90–91.
8. Carmel White, "Early Stone Axes in Arnhem Land," *Antiquity*, XLI, No. 162 (1967), 149–152.
9. Richard A. Gould, "Preliminary Report on Excavations at Puntutjarpa Rockshelter, near the Warburton Ranges, Western Australia" (with Appendices by D. Hackett, A. Glass, and R. Tedford), *Archaeology and Physical Anthropology in Oceania*, III, No. 3 (1968), 161–85. Carbon-14 dates received from Isotopes, Inc., of Westwood, New Jersey, March, 1968.
10. Gould, "Chipping Stones in the Outback," *op. cit.*
11. See Sollas, *op. cit.*, 244–46, 253, 337; also Herbert Basedow *The Australian Aboriginal* (Adelaide: F. W. Preece and Sons, Ltd., 1925), 15, 25–29.
12. Sherwood L. Washburn, "Thinking About Race," in *Readings in Anthropology*, E. A. Hoebel, J. D. Jennings, and E. R. Smith (eds.) (New York: McGraw-Hill Book Company, 1955), 108.
13. A. P. Elkin, *The Australian Aborigines* (New York: Doubleday and Company, Inc., 1964), 4.
14. *Ibid.*, 5.
15. Washburn, *op. cit.*, 106.
16. Quoted in Ronald M. and Catherine H. Berndt, *The World of the First Australians* (Sydney: Ure Smith, Ltd., 1964), 14–15.
17. H. H. Finlayson, *The Red Centre* (Sydney: Angus and Robertson, Ltd., 1935), 51.

18. Wilfred H. Douglas, "An Introduction to the Western Desert Language," *Oceania Linguistic Monograph* No. 4 (1964), 2.
19. Ronald M. Berndt, "The Concept of 'the Tribe' in the Western Desert of Australia," *Oceania*, XXX, No. 2 (1959), 85–86.
20. Mervyn J. Meggitt, "Aboriginal Food-Gatherers of Tropical Australia," *Proceedings and Papers of the IUCN 9th Technical Meeting*, No. 4, Part I (1964), 31. Also, for useful population figures see Joseph B. Birdsell, "Some Environmental and Cultural Factors Influencing the Structuring of Australian Aboriginal Populations," *American Naturalist*, LXXXVII, No. 834 (1953), 171–207.
21. Douglas, *op. cit.*, 3.
22. Edward Sapir, "Language," *Encyclopedia of the Social Sciences* (New York: The Macmillan Company, 1933), Vol. 9, 155.

CHAPTER 4: THE SATISFACTIONS OF SURVIVAL

1. Norman B. Tindale, "Legend of the Wati Kutjara, Warburton Range, Western Australia," *Oceania*, VII, No. 2 (1936), 184.
2. Harold S. Gladwin, *Men Out of Asia* (New York: McGraw-Hill Book Company, Inc., 1947), 52–53.
3. Donald F. Thomson, "The Bindibu Expedition," *The Geographical Journal*, Vol. 128, Part 3 (1962), 274.
4. James Deetz, *Invitation to Archaeology* (New York: The Natural History Press, 1967), 45.

CHAPTER 5: DESERT RITUALS AND THE SACRED LIFE

1. Norman B. Tindale, "Initiation among the Pitjandjara Natives of the Mann and Tomkinson Ranges of South Australia," *Oceania*, VI, No. 2 (1935), 199.
2. Of particular value are Spencer and Gillen, *The Native Tribes of Central Australia, op. cit.;* W. Baldwin Spencer and F. J. Gillen, *The Arunta* (London: Macmillan and Company, Ltd., 1927); W. E. H. Stanner, "On Aboriginal Religion," *Oceania Monograph No. 11* (1963); T. G. H. Strehlow, *Aranda Traditions* (Melbourne: Melbourne University Press, 1947); and Meggitt, *Desert People, op. cit.*
3. Emile Durkheim, *The Elementary Forms of the Religious Life* (New York: Collier Books, 1961), 52.

4. Ronald M. Berndt, "The Concept of 'the Tribe' . . . ," *op. cit.,* 97–98.

5. There is evidence that sometime between 1913 and 1930 the Aborigines living near Laverton and Mount Margaret Mission (and perhaps Warburton as well, later on) modified their original four-section system into the present six-section arrangement. The original system was described by Daisy M. Bates, "Social Organization of Some Western Australian Tribes," *Report of the Fourteenth Meeting of the Australasian Association for the Advancement of Science,* XIV (1913), 396–97. The later adjustments between groups which gave rise to the present six-section arrangement are described in detail by A. P. Elkin, "Kinship in South Australia," *Oceania,* X, No. 3 (1940), 298, 315–26.

6. R. M. and C. H. Berndt, *The World of the First Australians, op. cit.,* 60.

7. Douglas, *op. cit.,* 126.

8. The naming of "sun" and "shade" divisions by the Gibson Desert Aborigines is probably related in some way to the divisions "light-blooded"–"dark-blooded," light- and dark-color, "bloods and shades," and light- and dark-complexion, reported among Aboriginal societies from the eastern states of Australia and in the South Australian desert as far west as the area near the boundary of Western Australia. The occurrence of these named divisions is discussed by W. Baldwin Spencer, "Blood and Shade Divisions of Australian Tribes," *Proceedings of the Royal Society of Victoria,* XXXIV (1921–22), 1–6. The presence of these divisions is also mentioned by W. E. Harney, "Ritual and Behavior at Ayers Rock," *Oceania,* XXXI, No. 1 (1960), 63–64. In Harney's account the sun side is called Djindarlagul and the shade side Wumbularu—terms which are clearly cognate with the *tjiṇṭu* (sun) and *ngumpaluṛu* (shade) names for the two divisions used by the Ngatatjara and other Aborigines at Warburton.

   The easiest explanation for these two modes of expressing this division is to consider the "sun-shade" dichotomy as a sociocentric terminology and the system of alternating generations (*tarpuṭa-nganatarka*) as an egocentric terminology.

9. Meggitt, *Desert People, op. cit.,* 68.

10. This "double talk" is comparable in many ways to the ceremonial or "clowning" language of the Walbiri, called *tjiliwiri,* described by Kenneth Hale, "Language, Kinship, and Ritual among the Walbiri of Central Australia" (paper read at the annual meeting

of the American Anthropological Association, Washington, D.C., November 1967).

11. Tindale, "Initiation among the Pitjandjara Natives . . . ," *op. cit.,* 205.

12. Arnold van Gennep, *The Rites of Passage* (Chicago: University of Chicago Press, 1960), 75.

13. Géza Róheim, *The Eternal Ones of the Dream* (New York: International Humanities Press, 1945), 71–72, 74–75.

14. R. M. and C. H. Berndt, *The World of the First Australians, op. cit.,* 144–45.

15. Tindale, "Initiation among the Pitjandjara Natives . . . ," *op. cit.,* 222–23.

16. S. D. Porteus, "The Social Psychology of the Australian Aboriginal," *The Journal of Applied Psychology,* XIII, No. 2 (1929), 139.

17. Elkin, *op. cit.,* 175.

18. *Ibid.,* 176.

19. Strehlow, "Culture, Social Structure, and Environment in Aboriginal Australia," *op. cit.,* 132.

20. Tindale, "Initiation among the Pitjandjara Natives . . . ," *op. cit.,* 223.

21. Giles, *op. cit.,* I, 200.

22. Norman B. Tindale, "Musical Rocks and Associated Objects of the Pitjandjara People," *Records of the South Australian Museum,* XIV, No. 3 (1963), 500–1.

23. Meggitt, *Desert People, op. cit.,* 221.

24. R. M. and C. H. Berndt, *The World of the First Australians, op. cit.,* 209.

25. *Ibid.,* 183; also see discussion by Mervyn J. Meggitt, "Djanba among the Walbiri, Central Australia," *Anthropos,* L (1955), 398.

26. Max Gluckman, "The Logic of African Science and Witchcraft: An Appreciation of Evans-Pritchard's 'Witchcraft Oracles and Magic among the Azande,'" *Rhodes-Livingston Institute Journal* (June, 1944), 61–71.

27. Many of the terms and rituals associated with Tingari are cognate with those of the Gadjari cycle of the Walbiri, described by Mervyn J. Meggitt, "Gadjari among the Walbiri Aborigines of Central Australia," *Oceania Monograph No. 14* (1966), 32–33. The term Tingari applies both to the totemic beings themselves and the region from which they came. Gadjari and Tingari also have some similarities to the Kurangara cult of the Kimberleys, as reported by Helmut Petri, "Dynamik im Stammesleben Nordwest

Australiens," *Paideuma*, VI, No. 3 (1956), 152–68. Ngatatjara men at Warburton said that some of the Tingari rituals were like those of the Kuṛangara cult (of which they were aware, even though they had never themselves traveled that far north).

28. I have not said much in this chapter about the sorcerer as curer or about how he is trained and receives his powers. For a detailed account of these aspects of sorcery, see Ronald M. and Catherine H. Berndt, "A Preliminary Report of Field Work in the Ooldea Region, Western South Australia," *Oceania*, XIV, No. 1 (1943), 53–66. I did not investigate the matter of initiation and training of sorcerers in detail, but I did observe several cures by sorcerers at Warburton and Cundeelee and interviewed about them afterward I found that the curing practices among the *mapaṇtjara* (sorcerers) I witnessed and talked to were identical in most respects to those of the *kinkinba* (Ooldea word for sorcerers) described by the Berndts.

CHAPTER 6: ARTISTS AND MONUMENTS

1. R. J. C. Atkinson, *Stonehenge* (London: Hamish Hamilton, Ltd., 1956), 134–39.
2. Gerald S. Hawkins and John B. White, *Stonehenge Decoded* (New York: Dell Publishing Company, 1965).
3. André Leroi-Gourhan, "The Evolution of Paleolithic Art," *Scientific American*, Vol. 218, No. 2 (1968), 59–70.
4. *Ibid.*, 64–67.
5. Edward M. Curr, *The Australian Race* (Melbourne: John Ferres, Government Printer, 1886), I, 318–50.
6. Charles P. Mountford, *Ayers Rock* (Sydney: Angus and Robertson, Ltd., 1965).
7. R. M. and C. H. Berndt, in *The World of the First Australians, op. cit.*, 353, mention the presence of rock paintings at this place, which they call Wirindjara.
8. Giles, *op. cit.*, I, 267.
9. The carpet-snake dances witnessed in 1966 at Warburton as part of the Tingari cycle show several close similarities to the totemic python ritual of the Walbiri filmed at the sacred site of Ngama in Northern Territory (*Walbiri Ritual at Ngama*, Roger Sandall, director, film produced by the Australian Institute of Aboriginal Studies, Canberra, 1966, 23-1/2 minutes, color, sound, 16 mm).

10. More detailed accounts of this sacred tradition appear in R. M. and C. H. Berndt, *The World of the First Australians, op. cit.*, 208–209, and in Norman B. Tindale, "Totemic Beliefs in the Western Desert of Australia. Part I: Women Who Became the Pleiades," *Records of the South Australian Museum*, XIII, No. 3 (1959), 305–30.

11. Charles P. Mountford, *Aboriginal Paintings from Australia* (New York: Mentor-UNESCO Art Series, 1964), 12.

12. Robert Edwards, "Comparative Study of Rock Engravings of South and Central Australia," *Transactions of the Royal Society of South Australia*, Vol. 90 (1966), 33–41.

13. This point of view is shared by many archaeologists and art-historians and is expressed by John H. Rowe, "Archaeological Dating and Cultural Process," *Southwestern Journal of Anthropology*, XV, No. 4 (1959), 317–24.

CHAPTER 7: THE DISSATISFIED

1. Quoted in "The Outback Aborigines," *Current Affairs Bulletin*, XXIII, No. 3 (1958), 40.

2. R. M. and C. H. Berndt, *The World of the First Australians, op. cit.*, 438–39.

3. I am indebted to Samuel Mollenhauer, Acting Superintendent of the Warburton Ranges Mission during 1966, for first pointing out this fact to me and for additional information on family relationships among Aborigines residing at the Mission.

4. Meggitt, *Desert People, op. cit.*, 165.

5. R. M. and C. H. Berndt, *The World of the First Australians, op. cit.*, 58.

6. A few years ago the Western Australian Government took over from the Mission the function of running the school at Warburton. One of the most important results of this change was that Aborigine youngsters now live in camp with their families, instead of in dormitories at the Mission.

7. Fry, Henry Kenneth, "Kinship in Western Central Australia," *Oceania*, IV, No. 4 (1934), 473. In Fry's description of these equivalents some confusion is caused by the presence of a fifth section term (Purukula). I have found this term used by one young Aborigine from the Taltiwara region, but he and the others insist that it is a personal name only and does not refer

to a section. Since section and subsection terms are often used as personal names, it is easy to see how confusion might have arisen over this point at Mount Liebig. This term is probably related to the Purula subsection of the Aranda and may at one time have been a subsection in the Gibson Desert, though on present evidence this remains uncertain.

8. The census of June 30, 1967, reported that there are 454 full-blood Aborigines living in or near the Warburton Ranges Mission and 306 living at the Laverton Reserve.

9. The Government of Western Australia makes rations available to elderly Aborigines (declared, somewhat arbitrarily, "pensioners") and to Aborigine children in school.

10. This is a remarkably efficient service which operates throughout the Australian outback. It is subsidized in part by the Federal Government, though most of the expenses are met by private subscription. Remote missions and homesteads are provided with two-way radios and medical supplies, and the doctors are on call with their aircraft at several central bases. The ones nearest to the Gibson Desert are Meekatharra, Kalgoorlie, and Alice Springs. The organization was originally begun by the Australian Inland Mission of the Presbyterian Church, largely through the efforts of the late Very Reverend John Flynn, D.D.

11. Meggitt, *Desert People, op. cit.,* 77.

Glossary

ALTERNATING GENERATIONS. A dual division of society into two halves, each composed of individuals belonging to generation-levels which alternate with the levels of members of the opposite half. These divisions are a feature of the social organization of the Gibson Desert Aborigines. One division (one's own generation-level along with those of one's grandparents' and of one's grandchildren's) is called *nganatarka;* the other (the generation-levels of one's parents and children) is called *tarpuṭa.*

ARUNTA (ALSO CALLED ARANDA). Aborigines living in the vicinity of Alice Springs and the Macdonnell Ranges of Central Australia. Thanks to studies by Baldwin Spencer, F. J. Gillen, C. Strehlow, and T. G. H. Strehlow, the Aranda are one of the best-known Australian Aboriginal societies.

AUSTRALOPITHECUS. Genus of fossil hominids which appeared in Africa during the Early Pleistocene (around 2,000,000 to 1,500,000 years ago) according to recent evidence at the site of Olduvai Gorge in East Africa. These fossil hominids represent the first appearance of tool-using manlike creatures, some of which lead ultimately (though the fossil evidence is complex) to more modern forms of man.

BILLABONG. A colloquial Australian word describing a creek in which the water has ceased to flow but still lies in pools in the creek-bed.

BILLYCAN (OR BILLY). Colloquial Australian term for a large tin can (almost any shape will do), generally with a wire handle looped over the top, used to make tea while traveling in the bush.

BULLROARER. A sacred board attached to a cord of hair-string, which men twirl through the air at ceremonies to keep women and uninitiated men away.

CARPET SNAKE (*Morelia spilotes*). This non-poisonous snake belongs to the subfamily *Pythoninae* (pythons) and is called *tjikaṛi* by the Aborigines. It is edible.

CLASSIFICATORY KINSHIP. A system of kin terminology in which lineal relatives (for example, father, son) may be classed together by terms which also apply to certain collateral relatives; for example, father and father's brother may be addressed or spoken of by the same term. An important feature of Aboriginal social organization.

CULT-LODGES. Groups defined by the members' belief in common descent from a totemic ancestor (see Totemism). Among the Gibson Desert Aborigines this descent is in the male line. These groups act together in ritual affairs, including the custodianship of places where the ancestral being was active during the Dreamtime (*q.v.*).

DAMPER. A colloquial Australian expression for any unleavened loaf baked from a mixture of flour and water. This is standard fare for white Australians traveling in the bush.

DESERT OAK (*Casuarina decaisneana*). A tree quite unrelated to the true oaks, which thrives in sandplain and sandhill areas in the most remote parts of the Gibson Desert. The Aboriginal word for this tree is *kuṛkapi*.

DINGO. The Australian dog. Many are cared for by the Aborigines, with whom they live in a state of semidomestication, but others roam wild in the bush. The desert Aborigines call the domesticated dingo *papa* and the wild one *papa ngupanu*. Wild dingoes, as the only large carnivores in the Australian bush, have done much to reduce the numbers of indigenous marsupial fauna and are also detested by stockmen for the damage they do to livestock.

DREAMTIME (OR "DREAMING"). A sort of timeless time during which the totemic beings moved about the desert having adventures and performing creative acts. The specific localities at which these acts occurred are regarded as sacred by Aborigines today. The totemic spirits at these places are thought to be alive and influencing the present. The concept of the dreamtime, including the notion of places where dreamtime events occurred, is expressed in the word *tjukurpa*.

ECHIDNA. Australian spiny ant-eater (*Tachyglossus aculeatus*). This desert monotreme is easily recognized by its long snout and large spines. It is known to the Gibson Desert Aborigines as *tjilkamaṭa*.

EMU (*Dromaius novae-hollandiae*). This giant flightless bird is found throughout Australia. It is called *kalaya* by Pitjantjara-speaking Aborigines.

EURO (*Macropus robustus*). Sometimes called the wallaroo or hill kangaroo, this large marsupial closely resembles the common red or plains kangaroo (*Macropus rufus*) in appearance. The Ngatatjara word for euro is *kanyala*.

GHOST GUM (*Eucalyptus papuana*). A distinctive desert tree found growing mainly in and along creekbeds. It is notable for its smooth white bark.

GOANNA. Two species of this lizard commonly occur in the Gibson Desert: the Common Goanna (*Varanus varius*) and the one known colloquially as the Perentie Lizard (*V. giganteus*). Both species are hunted by the Aborigines, who call the former *kurkaṭi* and the latter *ngintaka*.

HAIR-BUN. See Pukutji.

HAIR-STRING. String fashioned from strands of human hair. In recent years rabbit fur has begun to be used in the same manner.

HORSEHOOF CORES. Large, discoidal stone cores from which flakes have been struck. These distinctively "hoof"-shaped artifacts occur at the earliest excavated levels of several very ancient archaeological sites in Australia.

KALAYA. See Emu.

KALPAṚI. Edible seeds of the shrub *Chenopodium rhadinostachyum*. This is an important staple food of the desert Aborigines when it ripens around April–May.

KAMPUṚARPA (*Solanum* species). A small edible green tomato-like fruit which ripens in the desert around July–August. It is a staple food of the Aborigines.

KUḶAṬA. Barbed throwing spear of the Gibson Desert Aborigines.

KUNMANARA. Name used as a circumlocution to avoid addressing someone by a name that sounds like that of a recently deceased person.

KUṆṬALA. A class of medium-sized sacred boards with a distinctive cylindrical shape. Incised designs consisting of concentric circles linked by lines commonly occur on these, with the circles representing the water sources visited by totemic beings in the dreamtime and the connecting lines representing the tracks of these beings as they traveled from one place to another.

KUPI-KUPI. A small whirlwind, sometimes called a willy-willy by white Australians.

KURKAṬI. See Goanna.

KURRAJONG (*Brachychiton* species). Called *ngalta* by the Aborigines, this tree is found in places throughout the desert and the mulga scrub of the desert fringe. Its edible seeds and water-bearing roots make it economically important to the Aborigines.

MALLEE. Communities of low trees dominated by *Eucalyptus* species. These plant communities occur scattered throughout the desert. The trees in them are distinctive in that the branches emanate upward from an underground stem or tuber rather than from an above-ground trunk.

MAMU. Spirits or ghosts which move about at night. Though opinions vary, mamu are usually thought to be cannibalistic and dangerous in other ways. The Aborigines believe that only a sorcerer can kill them or drive them away.

MANGURI. A circular pad, usually made of hair-string or emu feathers, used by a woman to balance and cushion loads she carries on her head.

MAPANPA. Objects, usually of some unusual substance such as quartz crystal or pearlshell, which a sorcerer (*mapantjara*) keeps in his "kit" ready to use in curing or against mamu.

MARSUPIAL CAT (*Dasyurinus geoffroyi*). Sometimes known colloquially as the "native cat," this medium-sized marsupial actually has little resemblance to the true cats. It is now almost extinct in the deserts of Australia. The desert Aborigines call this animal *partjata.*

MICROLITHS. A general term used by archaeologists to describe several varieties of small, carefully made stone tools. The small size of these tools suggests that they were hafted to handles of some kind in order to be used.

MINGKULPA (*Nicotiana excelsior*). A variety of true tobacco which grows wild in the Gibson Desert and is chewed as a mild narcotic by the Aborigines. Another species, *N. benthamiana* (called *tjunti-wari*), is also much sought after for the same purpose but is less common.

MOUNTAIN DEVIL (*Moloch horridus*). A bizarre-looking little lizard with sharp spines and patches of bright colors covering its body. It is perfectly harmless and is sometimes eaten by the desert Aborigines, who call it *ngiyari.*

MUKULPA. This term covers both the barb attached to the tip of a throwing-spear and the hook used to engage the spear at the end of a spearthrower.

MULATI (*Acacia dictyophleba*). A tree occurring in isolated parts of the Gibson Desert, with a thin and relatively straight stem suitable for making spears.

MULGA. Scrub vegetation characterized by the presence of *Acacia aneura* and other similar species of *Acacia*. Patches of such vegetation, some quite extensive, occur at various places throughout the Gibson Desert.

NANPA. A string belt made from strands of human hair.

NGARU (*Solanum eremophilum*). A shrub bearing a small, green tomato-like fruit which ripens around December–January. The fruit is a summer staple of the desert Aborigines.

NGATATJARA. A term denoting speakers of a particular dialect of the Pitjantjara language spoken by Aborigines living over a wide area centering on the Warburton Ranges. A variant spelling of this term, Ngadadjara, sometimes appears in the literature.

NGINTAKA. See Goanna.

NYATUNYATJARA. A term denoting speakers of a particular dialect of the Pitjantjara language spoken by a small number of people from a wide area roughly 100 to 200 miles north and northwest of the Warburton Ranges.

OUTBACK. A colloquial Australian term used to indicate any part of the country away from cities and other settlements—that is, most of Australia.

PALYKANPA. Bark sandals made by the Gibson Desert Aborigines, used to protect the feet from the heat of the sand during the summer months.

PEARLSHELL. Mother-of-pearl and other lustrous shell materials traded over long distances to the desert Aborigines from points along the coast (mainly in the north). Often the objects made from these shells are covered with ornate designs or carved into special shapes as pendants or pointing instruments.

PINTUPI. A loose term often used by anthropologists to designate the Aborigines living in parts of the Gibson and Great Sandy Deserts, all of whom speak various dialects of Pitjantjara. This term also appears in the literature as Pintubi, Bindibu, Bindaboo, Bindubi, Pintipu, and other variants.

PITJANTJARA (also called Pitjantjatjara). An Aboriginal language spoken over wide areas of the Victoria, Gibson, and Great Sandy Deserts. This is sometimes referred to in the literature as the Western Desert Language. Another common variant spelling in the literature is Pitjandjara.

PITJURU-PITJURU. A stone-tipped engraving tool with a wooden handle, used by the Gibson Desert Aborigines to incise sacred designs on wooden boards and spearthrowers.

PUKUTJI. The sacred hair-bun worn by circumcised men on ceremonial occasions.

ṚIṚA. An Aboriginal term denoting a landscape of low conglomerate knolls—the "great undulating desert of gravel" mentioned by Carnegie (see Bibliography).

ROCKSHELTER. A term used by archaeologists to denote a shallow natural cave—that is, a cave into which daylight penetrates.

SACRED BOARDS. Carved boards, generally elliptical in shape and varying in length from a few inches to as much as eight or nine feet, which are owned corporately by members of totemic cult-lodges and are displayed on ceremonial occasions. When not being carved or displayed these sacred items are kept in concealed caches. They generally have elaborate designs incised on their surfaces. The smallest are called *maṭaki;* medium-sized boards include *pakali, kuṇṭala,* and *yirilmaṛi;* while the largest are called *lara.* Some of the small to medium-sized boards have a hole drilled in one end. This is for attaching a hair-string cord when the board is to be used as a bullroarer (*q.v.*).

SECTIONS. Named categories in Aboriginal society which regulate marriage and facilitate long-distance visiting. Anthropologists designate Aboriginal groups with four or, in some cases (as at the Warburton Ranges), six of these categories as having sections, while groups with eight are said to possess subsections. The correlation of these categories with kinship relations and totemic groups in Australian Aboriginal societies is often exceedingly complex.

SPEARTHROWER. A device used by the desert Aborigines for a variety of purposes including that of a throwing-board or lever for propelling spears. It is called *langkuru* and *miru* by the Gibson Desert Aborigines.

SPINIFEX (*Triodia* species). A pale green, spiky grass growing in clumps of varying density throughout the central and western deserts of Australia. Some varieties yield edible seeds and another contains a resin (called *kiṭi*) which the Aborigines use as a general-purpose adhesive.

SUBINCISION. An extremely painful ordeal practiced by male Aborigines throughout the Gibson Desert; it involves cutting open the underside of the urethra.

TALIWANTI (*Crotalaria cunninghamii*). A desert shrub with tough, supple bark, used by the Gibson Desert Aborigines to make sandals.

TINGARI. A class of totemic beings said to have made their dreamtime travels in the desert region lying about 100 miles to the north of the Warburton Ranges. These beings include the carpet snake, eagle, a mythical water-snake, crow, and others.

TJAWU (*Acacia* species). A desert tree often called "gidgee" or "ironwood." It has fairly straight roots which the Aborigines use in making spearshafts.

TJUKURPA. See Dreamtime.

TOTEMISM. The close association of certain groups within a society with animate or inanimate beings (for example, animal and plant species). Throughout Aborigine Australia the relation of individuals and groups to particular totems is of great importance in social and ceremonial organization, although the particular forms of totemic relationship practiced by different societies vary tremendously.

WALBIRI. An Aboriginal tribe living over a wide area of desert country in Northern Territory, to the northwest of Alice Springs. Recent studies by M. J. Meggitt, K. Hale, and N. Munn have done much to describe the complexities of the language, art, and social organization of this important desert group.

WAMA. Sugar derived from a desert shrub (*Grevillea eriostachya*) with sweet and edible yellow flowers which the Aborigines either eat directly off the shrub or mix with water to make a sweet drink.

WANAMPI. The Pitjantjara word for the totemic water-snake, a mythological serpent known widely among Australian Aborigines by different names and characteristically associated with rain and water sources. Some anthropologists refer to it as the rainbow-snake.

WANGUNU (*Eragrostis eriopoda*). A grass from which the Aborigines gather the seeds around April-May. The seeds, ground into flour, mixed with water, and baked as a damper (*q.v.*), form a staple food of the Gibson Desert Aborigines.

WANIKI. Sacred string cross (in a wide variety of shapes and sizes) used by the desert Aborigines. The Pitjantjara word appears to be cognate with the Aranda term *waninga* for the same class of sacred paraphernalia.

WARMALA. A "war party" or group of kinsmen which sets out openly to avenge a wrong done to them, distinguished from a secret revenge party (called *tjinakarpil*) which covers its tracks by using emu-feather footpads and employs stealth and sorcery instead of fighting openly.

YIRILMAṚI. A sacred board with incised designs, used as a bullroarer and mnenonic device during ceremonies and as a pointing instrument to project illness and death by magical means.

YIWARΛ. Ngatatjara word for track.

Annotated Bibliography

This bibliography includes nearly all the available sources on the Gibson Desert Aborigines and their Pitjantjara-speaking neighbors. In cases where the subject is not made entirely clear by the title, a brief note identifies the subject and other relevant matters. Although the Pitjantjara-speaking peoples of Australia have been well studied, no compact and complete ethnographic study of this group has yet been made. As this bibliography shows, knowledge about these Aborigines is probably more varied and scattered than is the case for any other Aboriginal group in Australia.

ABBIE, A. A. "Metrical Characters of a Central Australian Tribe," *Oceania*, XXVII, No. 3, 1957, 220–243.

——— and ADEY, W. R. "Pigmentation in a Central Australian Tribe with Special Reference to Fair-Headedness," *American Journal of Physical Anthropology*, n.s. II, No. 3, 1953, 339–360.

——— and ADEY, W. R. "The Non-Metrical Characters of a Central Australian Tribe," *Oceania*, XXV, No. 3, 1955, 198–207.

BARRETT, CHARLES. "Dental Observations on Australian Aborigines, Yuendumu, Central Australia," *Australian Journal of Dentistry*, LVI, 1953, 128–138.

The preceding four papers describe physical characteristics of Ngalia and some Pintupi Aborigines at Yuendumu, Northern Territory.

BASEDOW, HERBERT. *The Australian Aboriginal*. Adelaide: F. W. Preece and Sons, Ltd., 1925.

A well-known work which includes information about Pitjantjara-speaking Aborigines in northwestern South Australia. Numerous photographs.

———. "Journal of the Government North-West Expedition," *Proceedings of the Royal Geographical Society of Australasia, South Australian Branch*, XV, 1914, 57–242.

General notes on Pitjantjara-speaking Aborigines encountered during 1903 expedition in northwestern South Australia. Numerous photographs.

BATES, DAISY M. "Social Organization of Some Western Australian Tribes," *Report of the Fourteenth Meeting of the Australasian Association for the Advancement of Science*, XIV, 1913, 387–400.
Includes description of section system of Aborigines in Laverton area. An important early source.

————. "Ooldea Water," *Proceedings of the Royal Geographical Society of Australasia, South Australian Branch*, XXI, 1919–20, 73–78.

————. *The Passing of the Aborigines*. London: John Murray, Ltd., 1938.

The preceding two works include firsthand accounts of conditions at Ooldea, South Australia, an important collecting point for Pitjantjara-speaking Aborigines from the Victoria Desert. Some of the conclusions (particularly about cannibalism) are open to question. A picture of early contact in this region, useful photographs included in both.

BEADELL, LEN. *Too Long in the Bush*. Adelaide: Rigby, Ltd., 1965.
————. *Blast the Bush*. Adelaide: Rigby, Ltd., 1967.
Popular accounts by engineer of the "Gunbarrel Highway." Include notes on Woomera Rocket Range, nuclear tests in South Australia, Aborigines and rock alignments encountered in Gibson Desert.

BERNDT, RONALD M. "Aboriginal Sleeping Customs and Dreams, Ooldea, South Australia," *Oceania*, X, No. 3, 1940, 286–294.

————. "Tribal Migrations and Myths Centering on Ooldea, South Australia," *Oceania*, XII, No. 1, 1941, 1–20.

————. "The Warburton Range Controversy," *Australian Quarterly*, XXIX, No. 2, 1957.

————. "The Concept of 'the Tribe' in the Western Desert of Australia," *Oceania*, XXX, No. 2, 1959, 81–107.
Describes totemic and social organization of Pitjantjara-speaking Aborigines. A detailed and important study.

————. "Two Love Magic Objects from Laverton, Western Australia," *Mankind*, V, No. 8, 1959, 363–64.

———— (ed.). *Australian Aboriginal Art*. London: Collier-Macmillan, Ltd., 1964.
Several survey articles, including one by T. G. H. Strehlow on art of the Central and Western Desert Aborigines. Color photographs.

——— and Berndt, Catherine H. "A Preliminary Report of Field Work in the Ooldea Region, Western South Australia," *Oceania Monograph*, 1945.

The closest thing to a complete Pitjantjara ethnography so far available. Describes social and ceremonial organization, women's life, language, sorcery, love magic, material culture, ordeals. Useful photographs of ceremonies.

——— and Berndt, Catherine H. *From Black to White in South Australia*. Melbourne: F. W. Cheshire, Ltd., 1951.

Describes changes among Aborigines due to white influence, includes chapter on Ooldea area, photographs.

——— and Berndt, Catherine H. "A Selection of Children's Songs from Ooldea, Western South Australia," *Mankind*, IV, No. 9, 1952, 364–76; No. 10, 1953, 423–34; No. 12, 1954, 501–508.

——— and Berndt, Catherine H. Summary Report: The University of Western Australia Anthropological Survey of the Eastern Goldfields, Warburton Range and Jigalong Areas. Mimeographed. Perth, 1957.

——— and Berndt, Catherine H. *The World of the First Australians*. Sydney: Ure Smith, Ltd., 1964.

A general survey of Australian Aborigines with many references to Pitjantjara-speaking Aborigines.

——— and Berndt, Catherine H. (eds.). *Aboriginal Man in Australia*. Sydney: Angus and Robertson, Ltd., 1965.

A series of papers on Aborigines, including important ones on the desert Aborigines by T. G. H. Strehlow, and on Walbiri marriage by M. J. Meggitt.

——— and Johnston, T. Harvey. "Death, Burial, and Associated Ritual at Ooldea, South Australia," *Oceania*, XII, No. 3, 1942, 189–208.

Black, J. M. "Language of the Everard Range Tribe," *Transactions of the Royal Society of South Australia*, Vol. 39 (1915), 732–35.

Breuil, Henri. "Observations sur les pierres taillées de la région d'Ooldea. Récoltées par Mrs. D. M. Bates," *Revue d'Ethnographie et des Traditions Populaires*, IV, 1923, 182–4.

Description, with drawings, of stone tools found near Ooldea.

British and Foreign Bible Society. *Tjukurpa Palja Markalu: The Gospel According to St. Mark in Pitjantjatjara*. Adelaide, 1949.

Brown, H. Y. L. "Report on Journey from Warrina to Musgrave Ranges," *South Australian Parliamentary Paper*, No. 45, 1890.

BUTEMENT, W. A. S., and PITHER, A. G. "Native Monument in Central Australia," *Antiquity,* 30, No. 118 (1956), 116.
Description of rock alignment in the Victoria Desert, with photographs.

CAMPBELL, T. D. "Observations on the Teeth of Australian Aborigines, Cockatoo Creek, Central Australia," *Australian Journal of Dentistry,* XLII, 1938, 44–47.

———— and HOSSFELD, P. S. "Australian Aboriginal Stone Arrangements in North-west South Australia," *Transactions of the Royal Society of South Australia,* XC, 1966, 171–76.
Description of alignments with sketches and photographs.

———— and LEWIS, A. J. "Aborigines of South Australia: Anthropometric, Descriptive, and Other Observations Recorded at Ooldea," *Transactions and Proceedings of the Royal Society of South Australia,* 1926, 183–91.

CANNING, A. W. "Report to the Secretary of Mines, Western Australia," Perth, 1907.
Describes pioneering of the Canning Stock Route, some notes on Aborigines.

CANNING, W. A. "Mr. Canning's Expeditions in Western Australia, 1906–7 and 1908–10," *Geographical Journal,* XXXVIII, No. 1, 1911, 26–29.
Summary of Canning's explorations, includes photographs and map. Brief mention of Aborigines, acknowledging their assistance to the expeditions.

CARNEGIE, DAVID W. *Spinifex and Sand.* New York: M. F. Mansfield and Co., 1898.
Narrative of Carnegie's 1896 explorations of the Gibson Desert; includes notes on Aborigines.

————. "On a Bark-Bundle of Native Objects from Western Australia," *Journal of the Royal Anthropological Institute,* I, n.s., 1899, 20–21.
Drawings and descriptions of sacred objects found in a bundle left by Aborigines at Family Well, a waterhole in the Great Sandy Desert.

CAWTHORNE, PETER. "An Aboriginal Site at Wiluna," *Western Australian Naturalist,* VIII, No. 6 (1963), 151–52.

CHRISTOPHERS, BARRY E. "The Aborigines of the Warburton Range," *Medical Journal of Australia,* December 7, 1957, 842.
Reply to W. S. Davidson, "Health and Nutrition of Warburton Range Natives" (*q.v.*).

CLELAND, JOHN BURTON. "Anthropological Expedition to Central Australia," *The Medical Journal of Australia*, December 19, 1931, 793.
General observations of Aborigines at Cockatoo Creek, Northern Territory.

————. "Pathological Lesions Met with Amongst the Aborigines in the Musgrave Ranges, South Australia," *Journal of Tropical Medicine (and Hygiene)*, XXXVII, No. 20, 1934, 305–11.

———— and JOHNSTON, T. HARVEY. "Notes on Native Names and Uses of Plants in the Musgrave Ranges Region," *Oceania*, VIII, No. 3, 1938, 208–342.

———— and JOHNSTON, T. HARVEY. "Blood Grouping of Aborigines in the North-West Portion of Central Australia, 1936 Series," *Journal of Tropical Medicine (and Hygiene)*, XLI, No. 2, 1938, 26–27.

———— and JOHNSTON, T. HARVEY. "Blood Grouping of Australian Aborigines at Ooldea, South Australia," *Journal of Tropical Medicine (and Hygiene)*, XLIV, No. 12, 1941, 76–78.

———— and TINDALE, NORMAN B. "The Ecological Surroundings of the Ngalia Natives in Central Australia and Native Names and Uses of Plants," *Transactions of the Royal Society of South Australia*, LXXVII, 1954, 81–86.

———— and TINDALE, NORMAN B. "The Native Names and Uses of Plants at Haast Bluff, Central Australia," *Transactions of the Royal Society of South Australia*, LXXXII, 1959, 123–40.

COTTON, B. C. (ed.). *Aboriginal Man in South and Central Australia, Part I*. Adelaide: Government Printer, 1966.
Collection including papers on physical characteristics by A. A. Abbie, intelligence testing by S. D. Porteus, and ecology and disease by J. B. Cleland.

CRAWFORD, IAN M. "An Aboriginal Meal," *Western Australian Naturalist*, X, No. 3 (1966), 69–71.
Describes faunal remains from surface of small Aboriginal camp in area southwest of the Bell Rock Range; makes deductions concerning diet.

————. "A Plan for Local Retention of Aboriginal Material," *Australian Institute of Aboriginal Studies Newsletter*, II, No. 7, 1968, 18–19.
Describes efforts to build secure storehouses for sacred objects at Laverton, Warburton, and other Aboriginal Reserves in Western Australia.

DAVIDSON, D. SUTHERLAND. "Notes on the Pictographs and Petroglyphs of Western Australia and a Discussion of Their Affinities Elsewhere on the Continent," *Proceedings of the American Philosophical Society,* XCVI, 1952, 76–117.

A detailed distributional survey of rock art including the western deserts of Australia. Davidson made other studies covering stone tools, spears, boomerangs, spearthrowers, rock alignments, and burial practices; but these are not included here, since they rely largely on primary sources which are cited.

DAVIDSON, W. S. "Health and Nutrition of Warburton Range Natives of Central Australia," *Medical Journal of Australia,* October 26, 1957, 801–805.

DEAN, BETH, and CARELL, VICTOR. *Dust for the Dancers.* New York: Philosophical Library, Inc., 1956.

Popular account of visits to Yuendumu, Haast Bluff, and Ernabella during a tour to design an Aboriginal-style ballet called "Corroboree." Describes several ceremonies. Color and black-and-white photographs.

DE GRAAF, M. "The Manufacture of Spinifex Gum by Desert Aborigines," *Western Australian Naturalist,* X, No. 5, 1967, 116–19.

"Desert Pintupi," *The Illustrated London News,* September 7, 1957, 371–73.

Popular account of patrols in the Gibson Desert led by E. C. Evans. Photographs.

DOUGLAS, WILFRED H. "Phonology of the Australian Aboriginal Language Spoken at Ooldea, South Australia," *Oceania,* XXV, No. 3, 1955, 216–29.

———. *Illustrated Topical Dictionary of the Western Desert Language, Warburton Ranges Dialect, Western Australia.* Perth: United Aborigines Mission, 1959.

Short but useful dictionary; entries not in alphabetical order.

———. "An Introduction to the Western Desert Language," *Oceania Linguistic Monograph,* No. 4, 1964.

The most complete and accurate grammar so far available. Also contains several texts and cultural notes.

———. "The Aborigines—Is a Balanced Approach Possible?" *Anthropological Forum,* I, No. 2, 1964, 248–57.

Describes recent work and aims of missions in the Gibson and Victoria Deserts. Includes notes on Warburton Mission.

DUGUID, CHARLES. "Aborigines and the Rocket Range," *Australian Board of Missions Review,* August 1, 1947, 122–24.

EDWARDS, ROBERT. "Comparative Study of Rock Engravings of South and Central Australia," *Transactions of the Royal Society of South Australia,* XC, 1966, 33–41.
Includes detailed description of rock engravings at Tukulnga, Northern Territory, with photographs and ethnographic notes from Pitjantjara informants.

ELKIN, A. P. "Studies in Australian Totemism: Sub-section, Section, and Moiety Totemism," *Oceania,* IV, No. 1, 1933, 65–90.

————. "Studies in Australian Totemism: The Nature of Australian Totemism," *Oceania,* IV, No. 2, 1933, 1–131.
The two preceding papers are a detailed survey, which includes Pitjantjara-speaking Aborigines.

————. "Beliefs and Practices Connected with Death in North-Eastern and Western South Australia," *Oceania,* VII, No. 3, 1937, 275–99.

————. "Kinship in South Australia," *Oceania,* VIII, No. 4, 1938, 419–452; IX, No. 1, 1938, 41–78; X, No. 2, 1939, 198–234; X, No. 3, 1940, 295–399; X, No. 4, 1940, 369–89.
The title is misleading, since these papers deal in detail with social organization of Pitjantjara-speakers in South and Western Australia. An important source based on much firsthand work.

————. "Guided Projectiles and the Welfare of the Aborigines," *Australian Board of Missions Review,* July 1, 1947, 102–103.

————. *The Australian Aborigines.* New York: Doubleday and Co., Inc., 1964.
Includes references to and pictures of Pitjantjara Aborigines.

ELPHINSTONE, J. J. "Report on Health and Nutrition of Natives from Rawlinson Range to Lake Macdonald," Perth (1958).
Includes a list of Aboriginal plant foods by W. H. Moyle.

EVANS, E. C., and LONG, J. P. M. "The Aborigines of Western Central Australia," *The Geographical Journal,* CXXXI, Part 3, 1965, 318–29.
Describes patrols in Gibson Desert, 1957–1964.

FINLAYSON, H. H. *The Red Centre.* Sydney: Angus and Robertson, 1935.
Popular account by a zoologist of his travels in the Rawlinson and Petermann Ranges in the early 1930s. Observations and photographs of Aborigines.

FORREST, JOHN. *Explorations in Australia.* London: Sampson Low, Marston, Low, and Searle, 1875.

FRASER, MALCOLM A. C. "Aborigines of Western Australia," in his

Notes on the Natural History of Western Australia, Perth: Government Printer, 1903, 64–79.
Includes notes and a photograph of Aborigines near Laverton.

FRY, HENRY KENNETH. "Body and Soul: A Study from Western Central Australia," *Oceania,* III, No. 3, 1933, 247–56.
Discussion of totemism among Ngalia and Pintupi Aborigines studied near Mount Liebig, Northern Territory, in 1932.

———. "Kinship in Western Central Australia," *Oceania,* IV, No. 4, 1934, 472–78.
Describes the eight-subsection system operating in Mount Liebig area in 1932 (discusses same section names but different marriage and descent rules from system to north of Warburton) and mentions equivalents between section and subsection terminology. Includes summary of kinship terms.

GILES, ERNEST. *Australia Twice Traversed.* 2 vols. London: Sampson Low, Marston, Searle, and Rivington, Ltd., 1889.

GLASS, AMY, and HACKETT, DOROTHY. Pitjantjatjara Texts. Manuscript (1968) on file at the Australian Institute of Aboriginal Studies, Canberra.
The best available collection of texts in this language; all collected in the Ngatatjara dialect. To be published by the Australian Institute of Aboriginal Studies.

GOSSE, WILLIAM. "Report on Expedition of 1873," *South Australian Parliamentary Paper,* No. 48, Adelaide, 1874.

GOULD, ELIZABETH B. "Living with the Aborigines," *Nature and Science,* VI (1968), No. 2, 5–7; No. 3, 2–4.
Descriptive account of personal experiences and traditional food-collecting among the Gibson Desert Aborigines, written for children. Several photographs.

GOULD, RICHARD A. "Notes on Hunting, Butchering, and Sharing of Game among the Ngatatjara and their Neighbors in the West Australian Desert," *Kroeber Anthropological Society Papers,* No. 36 (1967), 41–66.

———. "Masculinity and Mutilation in a Primitive Society," *Medical Opinion and Review,* IV, No. 1 (1968), 58–75.
Brief review of physical ordeals in Ngatatjara society; photographs.

———. "Chipping Stones in the Outback," *Natural History,* LXXVII, No. 2 (1968), 42–49.
Manufacture and use of stone tools by desert Aborigines; color and black-and-white photographs.

———. "Living Archaeology: The Ngatatjara of Western Australia," *Southwestern Journal of Anthropology*, XXIV, No. 2 (1968), 101–122.
A "grammar" of archaeological behavior, including rock art, stone alignments, campsites, stone tools, etc., of the Gibson Desert Aborigines.

———. "Preliminary Report on Excavations at Puntutjarpa Rockshelter, near the Warburton Ranges, Western Australia," *Archaeology and Physical Anthropology in Oceania*, III, No. 3 (1968), 161–85.
Includes notes on stone technology and Ngatatjara texts collected and translated by D. Hackett and A. Glass, several photographs.

——— and GOULD, ELIZABETH B. "Kunturu, an Aboriginal Sacred Site on Lake Moore, Western Australia," *American Museum Novitiates*, No. 2327 (1968), 1–17.

GRAYDEN, WILLIAM L. "Report of the Select Committee Appointed to Inquire into the Native Welfare Conditions in the Laverton–Warburton Range Area." Perth, 1956.

GREENWAY, JOHN. "We Are All Aborigines in a New World," *New York Times Magazine*, November 10, 1968, 30–140.
Disjointed popular account of Aboriginal acculturation in Australia; includes notes on Ernabella, Laverton, and Warburton Ranges.

HACKETT, CECIL J. "Man and Nature in Central Australia," *The Geographical Magazine*, IV, No. 4 (1937), 287–98.
Popular article describing Aborigines in Musgrave Range area; numerous photographs.

HANSEN, IAN V. "An Account of the Ngalia Initiation Ceremonies at Yuendumu, Central Australia," *Transactions of the Royal Society of South Australia*, LXXVII (1954), 175–81.

HARNEY, W. E. "Ritual and Behavior at Ayers Rock," *Oceania*, XXXI, No. 1 (1960), 63–76.
Brief description of totemic geography at Ayers Rock.

HELMS, RICHARD. "Anthropology of the Elder Exploring Expedition," *Transactions of the Royal Society of South Australia*, XVI (1896), 237–332.
The first detailed description of Aborigines living in area east and south of the Warburton Ranges; includes photographs, drawings, vocabularies.

HILLIARD, WINIFRED. *The People in Between: The Pitjantjatjara People of Ernabella.* London: Hodder and Stoughton, Ltd., 1968.
Detailed history of the Ernabella Mission, with notes on the Aborigines, by a missionary who has done much to develop craft skills as an economic activity for missionized Aborigines.

HOLMES, CHARLES H. "Rockets over Australia," *Walkabout,* XIII (November, 1946), 6–16.
Arguments about the Woomera Rocket Range.

IDRIESS, ION L. *Lasseter's Last Ride.* Sydney: Angus and Robertson, Ltd., 1931.
Popular account of disastrous prospecting expeditions into Gibson Desert. Photographs and remarks about Aborigines.

JOHNSON, J. E. "Observations on Some Aboriginal Campsites in South Australia and Adjoining States," *Mankind,* VI, No. 2 (1963), 64–79; VI, No. 4 (1964), 154–81.
Surface collections of stone tools and site descriptions in northwestern South Australia and Western Australia east of the Warburton Ranges; drawings.

JOHNSTON, T. HARVEY. "Some Aboriginal Routes in the Western Portion of South Australia," *Proceedings of the Royal Geographical Society of Australasia, South Australian Branch,* XLII (1941), 33–65.

———— and CLELAND, J. BURTON. "Aboriginal Names and Uses of Plants in the Ooldea Region, South Australia," *Transactions of the Royal Society of South Australia,* LXVI (1942), 93–103.

JONES, FREDERIC WOOD. "The Ordered Arrangement of Stones Present in Certain Parts of Australia," *Journal of the Royal Anthropological Institute,* LV (1925), 123–28.
Describes rock alignments in western South Australia; photographs.

LEEDING, V. J. Notes on the Pintubi Dialect of the Western Desert Language. Manuscript (1966), on file at Australian Institute of Aboriginal Studies, Canberra.

LINDGREN, ERIC. "Aboriginal Rock Paintings near Jigalong," *Western Australian Naturalist,* VII, No. 5 (1960), 125–28.

————. "Aboriginal Flora and Fauna Names from Jigalong," *Western Australian Naturalist,* VII, No. 8 (1961), 195–201.

Two papers with useful notes on Aborigines from the western edge of the Gibson Desert.

LINDSAY, DAVID. *Journal of the Elder Scientific Exploring Expedition, 1891–2.* Adelaide: Government Printer, 1893.
Some notes on Aborigines encountered during the expedition. Vocabularies by L. A. Wells.

LOCKWOOD, DOUGLAS. *The Lizard Eaters.* Melbourne: Cassel Australia, Ltd., 1964.
Popular account by a journalist accompanying a 1963 government patrol into the Gibson Desert; includes photographs.

LONG, J. P. M. "Preliminary Work in Planning Welfare Development in the Petermann Ranges," *Australian Territories,* III, No. 2 (1963), 4–12.
Useful account of white contact and welfare efforts at Areyonga and other localities in Northern Territory, photographs.

———. "The Pintupi Patrols: Welfare Work with the Desert Aborigines," *Australian Territories,* IV, No. 5 (1964), 43–48; IV, No. 6 (1964), 24–35.

LOVE, J. R. B. "A Primitive Method of Making a Wooden Dish by Native Women of the Musgrave Ranges, South Australia," *Transactions of the Royal Society of South Australia,* LXVI (1942), 215–17.

———. "The Pronoun in Worora and Pitjantjatjara," *Oceania,* XVI, No. 1 (1945), 70–78.

———. "Percussion Flaking of Adze Blades in the Musgrave Ranges," *Mankind,* IV, No. 7 (1951), 297–8.

——— and TRUDINGER, R. M. *Tjukurpa Palja Markaku: The Gospel According to St. Mark in Pitjantjatjara.* Sydney, 1949.

"Man at His Most Primitive: The Bindibu of Australia Still Live in the Stone Age," *Life,* XLIV, No. 20 (May 19, 1958), 52–58.
Popular article, several photographs.

MANN, IDA. "Report on Opthalmic Findings in Warburton Range Aborigines of Central Australia," *Medical Journal of Australia,* October 26, 1957, 810–12.

MATHEWS, A. G. "The Preparation of Spinifex Gum by Australian Aborigines (Warburton Ranges), *Western Australian Naturalist,* IX, No. 4 (1964), 96.

MAY, E. and WILD, S. "Aboriginal Music on the Laverton Reservation, Western Australia," *Ethnomusicology,* XI, No. 2 (1967), 207–17.

McCARTHY, FREDERICK D. *Australian Aboriginal Stone Implements.* Sydney: The Australian Museum, 1967.

An up-to-date survey of Aboriginal stone tools, including desert types; photographs and drawings.

MEGGITT, MERVYN J., "The Bindibu and Others," *Man*, LXI, Article No. 172 (1961), 143.
A rejoinder to articles by Donald Thomson on bark sandals and tobacco among the desert Bindibu.

MITCHELL, S. R. *Stone Age Craftsmen*. Melbourne: Tait Book Co., Ltd., 1949.
Describes stone tools and campsites of Aborigines, including a site near Wiluna, on the western fringe of the Gibson Desert.

MOUNTFORD, CHARLES P. "Aboriginal Crayon Drawings II: Relating to Totemic Places in South Western Central Australia," *Transactions of the Royal Society of South Australia*, LXI (1937), 226–40.

———. "Rock Paintings at Windulda, Western Australia," *Oceania*, VII, No. 4 (1937), 429–35.
Paintings in caves about 50 miles southwest of Warburton Ranges Mission.

———. "Gesture Language of the Ngada Tribe of the Warburton Ranges, Western Australia," *Oceania*, IX, No. 2 (1938), 152–55.

———. "Aboriginal Crayon Drawings from the Warburton Ranges in Western Australia Relating to the Wanderings of the Two Ancestral Beings the Wati Kutjara," *Records of the South Australian Museum*, VI, No. 1 (1937), 5–28.

———. "A Contrast in Drawings Made by Australian Aborigines Before and After Initiation," *Records of the South Australian Museum*, VI, No. 2 (1938), 111–14.

———. "Aboriginal Crayon Drawings III: The Legend of Wati-Jula and the Kunkerunkara Women," *Transactions of the Royal Society of South Australia*, LXII (1938), 241–54.

———. "Aboriginal Crayon Drawings, Warburton Ranges, Western Australia," *Oceania*, X, No. 1 (1939), 73–79.

———. "Aboriginal Crayon Drawings IV: Relating to Everyday Incidents of the Ngada Tribe of the Warburton Ranges of Western Australia," *Transactions of the Royal Society of South Australia*, LXIII (1939), 3–13.

———. "An Unrecorded Method of Manufacturing Wooden Implements by Simple Stone Tools," *Transactions of the Royal Society of South Australia*, LXV (1941), 312–16.

———. "Modern Stone Age Men in South Australia; the Pitjendara Tribe," *Nature* (London), CXLIX (June 6, 1942), 641.

———. "Earth's Most Primitive People: Journey with the Aborigines of Central Australia," *National Geographic Magazine,* LXXXIX (1946), 89–112.
Popular article with color and black-and-white photographs.

———. *Brown Men and Red Sand.* Sydney: Angus and Robertson, Ltd., 1962.
Popular book about desert Aborigines in northwestern South Australia; photographs.

———. "Sacred Objects of the Pitjandjara Tribe, Western Central Australia," *Records of the South Australian Museum,* XIV, No. 2 (1962), 397–411.

———. *Ayers Rock.* Sydney: Angus and Robertson, Ltd., 1965.
Popular but detailed account of sacred traditions and rock paintings at Ayers Rock and Mount Olga. Includes general notes on Aborigines, correct except for items about marriage. Black-and-white and color photographs; drawings.

——— and CAMPBELL, T. D. "Aboriginal Arrangement of Stones in Central Australia," *Transactions of the Royal Society of South Australia,* LXIII (1939), 17–21.

NOONE, H. V. V. "Some Aboriginal Stone Implements of Western Australia," *Records of the South Australian Museum,* VII, No. 3 (1943), 271–80.
Description of surface collections including some from along Canning Stock Route.

"Outback Aborigines, The," *Current Affairs Bulletin,* XXIII, No. 3 (1958), 34–48.
A review of problems in acculturation and government policies toward Aborigines. Periodical published by the University of Sydney.

PREISS, K. A. "Aboriginal Implements from Ayers Rock," *The South Australian Naturalist,* XXXIII, No. 3 (1959), 44–45.
Meager description of surface-collected stone tools; no illustrations.

PRINGLE, L. A. B., and KOLLOSCHE, H. E. "Preliminary Notes on Aboriginal Paintings, Carved Stones, Arranged Stones and Stone Structures in the Mt. Olga Region of Central Australia," *Transactions of the Royal Society of South Australia,* LXXXI (1958), 131–40.

REAY, MARIE (ed.). *Aborigines Now.* Sydney: Angus and Robertson, Ltd., 1964.
Collection of papers, including useful articles by N. Munn on Wal-

biri art and J. P. M. Long on conditions at Papunya Reserve, Northern Territory.

ROBINSON, ROLAND. *The Feathered Serpent.* Sydney: Edwards and Shaw, Ltd., 1956.
Includes heavily edited versions of the Yula and Bush-turkey myths of the Pitjantjara.

"Rockets' Path," *Newsweek,* XXIX (March 17, 1947), 44.
Comments on the Woomera Rocket Range.

RÓHEIM, GÉZA. "Psychoanalysis of Primitive Cultural Types," *International Journal of Psychoanalysis,* XIII, Parts 1 and 2 (1932), 1–224.
Psychoanalytic interpretations of Aboriginal ordeals, rituals, and sexual practices, includes Ngatatjara and Pintupi informants. Photographs.

————. "Women and Their Life in Central Australia," *Journal of the Royal Anthropological Institute,* LXIII (1933), 209–65.
Useful notes on women's activities and beliefs; several Ngatajara and Pitjantjara-speaking informants are included in study.

————. *The Eternal Ones of the Dream.* New York: International Universities Press, 1945.
Psychoanalytic interpretations of the sacred life. Concentrates on Aranda, but includes some Ngatatjara and Pitjantjara-speaking Aborigines in study. Proposes several important theories.

ROSE, FREDERICK G. G. *The Wind of Change in Central Australia.* Berlin: Deutsche Akademie der Wissenschaften zu Berlin, 1965.
A 1962 study of recent economic and social changes among Pitjantjara Aborigines at Angas Downs, Central Australia.

ROSE, RONALD. *Living Magic.* New York: Rand McNally and Co., 1956.
Account of studies in extrasensory perception (E.S.P.) carried out by two students of J. B. Rhine at Areyonga in Northern Territory. Includes anecdotal experiences with Pitjantjara Aborigines and photographs.

ROWLANDS, R. J., and ROWLANDS, J. M. "Some Aboriginal Wells in the Western Desert of Australia," *Mankind,* VI, No. 5 (1965), 231–37.
Locations and description of native soak-holes in the Gibson Desert, photographs.

————. "Aboriginal Stone Arrangements in the Western Desert of Australia," *Mankind,* VI, No. 8 (1966), 355–58.
Brief description with sketches and photographs of rock alignment near the Dovers Hills in the Gibson Desert.

SCOTT, D., and SCOTT, M. K. "Blood Groups of Some Australian Aborigines of the Western Desert," *Nature* (London), October 26, 1966, 212.

SHEARD, LAURI E. *An Australian Youth among Desert Aborigines.* Adelaide: Libraries Board of South Australia, 1964.
Posthumously published field diary of studies made of Pitjantjara Aborigines in Ernabella–Musgrave Range area in 1940. Contains useful details and photographs.

SOFOULIS, JOHN. "Water Supplies, Warburton Range and Adjoining Areas," *Report of the Geological Survey Branch for 1961,* Perth (1962), 13–15.
Geological description of several important native rockholes, including assessment of their water-holding capacities. Photographs.

STANNER, W. E. H., and SHEILS, H. (eds.). *Australian Aboriginal Studies.* London: Oxford University Press, 1963.
A stocktaking of anthropological results and of areas urgently in need of work. Papers of 1961 Research Conference at the Australian Institute of Aboriginal Studies. Includes useful papers by R. M. Berndt on groups with minimal contact and in need of study, especially in and near the Gibson Desert.

STREHLOW, C., and VON LEONHARDI, M. *Die Aranda- und Loritja Stämme in Zentral Australien. Mythen, Sagen, und Märchen des Aranda-Stämmes in Zentral Australien.* Frankfurt: Veröffentlichungen des Frankfurter Museums fur Völkerkunde, 1907–1921.
A standard work on the Aranda, with references to their Pitjantjatjara-speaking neighbors.

STREHLOW, T. G. H. "Aboriginal Language, Religion, and Society in Central Australia," *Australian Territories,* II, No. 1 (1962), 4–11.
Popular but detailed account of personal career and life among desert Aborigines, including Pitjantjara-speakers; several photographs.

TERRY, MICHAEL. *Across Unknown Australia.* London: Herbert Jenkins, Ltd., 1925.
Popular account of travels through the Gibson Desert by motorcar. A few references to Aborigines.

———. "Explorations near the Border of Western Australia," *Geographical Journal,* LXXXIV (1934), 498–510.

———. *Sand and Sun.* London: Michael Joseph, Ltd., 1937.
Popular account of two prospecting trips from Lake Mackay to

the Warburton Ranges in 1932, looking for Lasseter's Reef (a ru-
mored gold deposit). Little about Aborigines; a few photographs.

THOMSON, DONALD F. *The Aborigines and the Rocket Range.* Melbourne: 1947.

————. "A Bark Sandal from the Desert of Central Western Australia," *Man,* LX, Article No. 228 (1960), 177–79.

————. "A Narcotic from *Nicotiana Ingulba,* used by the Desert
Bindibu," *Man,* LXI, Article No. 2 (1961), 5–8.

————. "The Bindibu Expedition," *The Geographical Journal,*
CXXVIII, Parts I–III (1962), 1–14; 143–57; 262–78.

————. "Some Wood and Stone Implements of the Bindibu Tribe of
Central Western Australia," *Proceedings of the Prehistoric Society
for 1964,* n.s. XXX (1964), 400–22.

The four preceding references contain detailed ethnographic information from expeditions conducted in 1957 near Lake Hazlett,
in the northern part of the Gibson Desert; many useful photographs
and descriptions.

TINDALE, NORMAN B. "Initiation among the Pitjandjara Natives of the
Mann and Tomkinson Ranges in South Australia," *Oceania,* VI, No.
2 (1935), 199–224.

————. "General Report on the Anthropological Expedition to the Warburton Range, Western Australia, July–September, 1935," *Oceania,*
VI, No. 4 (1936), 481–85.

————. "Legend of the Wati Kutjara, Warburton Range, Western
Australia," *Oceania,* VII, No. 2 (1936), 169–85.

————. "Natives of the Western Desert of Australia," *Man,* XXXVII,
(1937), 33.
Brief note on ethnographic films made in Mann Range, South
Australia.

————. Vocabulary of Pitjandjara. The Language of the Natives of
the Great Western Desert. Manuscript (1937), on file at South Australian Museum, Adelaide.

————. "A Game from the Great Western Desert of Australia," *Man,*
XXXVIII, Article No. 145 (1938), 128–29.

————. "Distribution of Australian Aboriginal Tribes: A Field Survey," *Transactions of the Royal Society of South Australia,* LXIV
(1940), 140–231.
The most thorough attempt so far at a tribal map of Australia,
with notes on names and locations of each group. Includes Gibson

Desert area, but the boundaries and some of the names used there are open to question.

———. "A List of Plants Collected in the Musgrave and Mann Ranges, South Australia," *South Australian Naturalist*, XXI, No. 1 (1941), 8–12.
Includes notes on Aboriginal names and uses, one photograph.

———. "The Hand Axe Used in the Western Desert of Australia," *Mankind*, III, No. 2 (1941), 37–41.
Describes Ngatatjara man using stone handax in Warburton Ranges; includes a photograph and drawings.

———. "Survey of the Half-Caste Problem in South Australia," *Proceedings of the Royal Geographical Society of Australasia*, XLII (1941), 66–161.
Includes a general discussion of demography and factors arising from white contact at the Warburton Ranges and Mount Margaret Missions.

———. "Totemic Beliefs in the Western Desert of Australia, Part I: Women Who Became the Pleiades," *Records of the South Australian Museum*, XIII, No. 3 (1959), 305–30.

———. "Musical Rocks and Associated Objects of the Pitjandjara People," *Records of the South Australian Museum*, XIV, No. 3 (1963), 499–514.

———. "Stone Implement Making among the Nakako, Ngadadjara and Pitjandjara of the Great Western Desert," *Records of the South Australian Museum*, XV, No. 1 (1965), 131–64.

——— and HACKETT, CECIL J. "Preliminary Report on Field Work among the Aborigines of the North-west of South Australia, May 31st to July 30th, 1933," *Oceania*, IV, No. 1 (1933), 101–105.

——— and LINDSAY, H. A. *Aboriginal Australians*. Brisbane: Jacaranda Press, Ltd., 1963.
Popular book on Aborigines, includes references to Pitjantjara and photographs of people at Mount Liebig, Warburton Ranges, and Mann Range.

TONKINSON, ROBERT. Gadudjara Vocabulary: A Dialect of the Western Desert Language. Manuscript (1965), on file in Department of Anthropology, University of Western Australia, Perth.

TRUDINGER, RONALD M. "Grammar of the Pitjantjatjara Dialect, Central Australia," *Oceania*, XIII, No. 3 (1943), 205–23.

WARBURTON, PETER EGERTON. *Journey Across the Western Interior of Australia.* London, 1875.

WELLS, L. A. "Abstract of Journal of Explorations in Western Australia, 1896–1897," *Proceedings of the Royal Geographical Society of Australasia, South Australian Branch,* III (1888–1898), 149–71.
Brief notes on Aborigines in area north of Lake Percival.

—— and GEORGE, F. R. "Prospecting Operations in the Musgrave, Mann, and Tomkinson Ranges," *South Australian Parliamentary Paper No. 54,* Adelaide (1904).

WESTERN AUSTRALIA DEPARTMENT OF NATIVE WELFARE. "The Central Australian Aboriginal Reserves." Perth (1965).
Brief notes on geography, missions, government stations, and Aborigines. Includes photographs and notes on Gibson Desert.

——. "A Place in the Sun." Perth (1968).
Describes recent efforts at assimilation of Aborigines in Western Australia; includes census figures for 1967.

WHITE, SAMUEL A. "Aborigines of the Everard Range," *Transactions and Proceedings of the Royal Society of South Australia,* XXXIX (1915), 725–32.

YENGOYAN, ARAM A. "A Comparison of Certain Marriage Features between the Pitjandjara and Other Groups of the Western Desert with the Northern Groups; also Some Comments on the Red Ochre Ceremonies," *Journal of the Anthropological Society of South Australia,* V, No. 4 (1967), 16–19.

—— "Demographic and Ecological Influences on Aboriginal Australian Marriage Sections," in Lee, Richard B., and DeVore, Irven (eds.), *Man the Hunter.* Chicago: Aldine Press, 1968.
Includes discussion of demography and marriage sections in the Gibson Desert area.

FILMS AND RECORDINGS

The Pitjantjara-speaking people of Australia have been filmed extensively and much of their music has been recorded. For a complete listing of anthropological films up to 1959 see John Greenway, *Bibliography of the Australian Aborigines and the Native Peoples of Torres Straits* (Sydney: Angus and Robertson, Ltd., 1963); listings appear under the names of E. O. Stocker, N. B. Tindale, C. P. Mountford, H. K. Fry, and T. D. Campbell. This book also lists phonograph records of desert Aborigine music by A. P. Elkin and J. Villeminot. For a more recent survey of ethnographic films see Ian Dunlop (ed.), *Retrospective Review of Australian Ethnographic Films, 1901–1967* (Sydney: Australian Commonwealth Film Unit, 1967), which lists early films made by W. Baldwin Spencer and recent efforts such as those by I. Dunlop, T. G. H. Strehlow, and R. Sandall.

Acknowledgments

Thanks are due to many institutions and individuals that have been of real assistance in the research and preparation leading up to this book. The fieldwork was carried out on a grant from the Social Science Research Council (U.S.A.), with additional funds for the Land-Rover from the Australian Institute of Aboriginal studies (Canberra) and funds for collecting artifacts supplied by the American Museum of Natural History.

Special thanks are owed to the following persons for their many courtesies and material assistance to this research: Dr. Ronald M. Berndt, Dr. Catherine H. Berndt, and Mrs. Thyra Robertson of the Department of Anthropology, University of Western Australia; Frank Gare, Glen Cornish, David Kininmonth, Lloyd Fletcher, and Stan Bridgeman of the Western Australian Department of Native Welfare; Ron Roberts and Robert Verburgt of the Weapons Research Establishment (Woomera); Robert Hewitt of the Western Mining Corporation, Ltd.; Samuel Mollenhauer, Richard Hawthorne, Amy Glass, Dorothy Hackett, and the Nursing Sisters at the Warburton Ranges Mission; Dr. W. D. L. Ride, Ian Crawford, and Sara Meagher of the Western Australian Museum.

Before my wife and I set out for the desert we received useful advice from many individuals, in particular from Robert Tonkinson, Norman Tindale, Dr. Mervyn Meggitt, Harry Butler, and Mark de Graaf. I am grateful to Dr. Margaret Mead, Dr. Harry L. Shapiro, and Hobart Van Deusen for reading and criticizing the manuscript; to Nicholas Amorosi for his painstaking art work; to the American Museum of Natural History for the assistance rendered by its photographic, library, and other facilities; and to the magazines *Natural History, Nature and Science,* and *Medical Opinion and Review* for allowing me to use in the book certain photographs which had first appeared in these publications.

Above all, I am grateful to the Aborigines who helped us in our studies, most of whom are mentioned by name in the book. Special thanks also go to Paul Porter, Ivan Shepherd, and Andrew Lawson, whose good cheer and reliability as our guides were much appreciated.

Index

About the Author

RICHARD A. GOULD was born in Newton, Massachusetts, and received his B.A. in Anthropology (*cum laude*) in 1961 from Harvard College and his Ph.D. in Anthropology from the University of California in 1965. He has been awarded a graduate fellowship by the National Science Foundation and a postdoctoral fellowship by the Social Science Research Council. Dr. Gould has made archaeological excavations in the Glen Canyon, Utah, and done combined archaeological and ethnographic studies in northwestern California, largely among the Tolowa Indians of that region. He is now Assistant Curator of North American Archaeology at the American Museum of Natural History in New York City. A fellow of the American Anthropological Association and a member of numerous societies, including the Australian Institute of Aboriginal Studies, Dr. Gould lives with his wife in New York City.

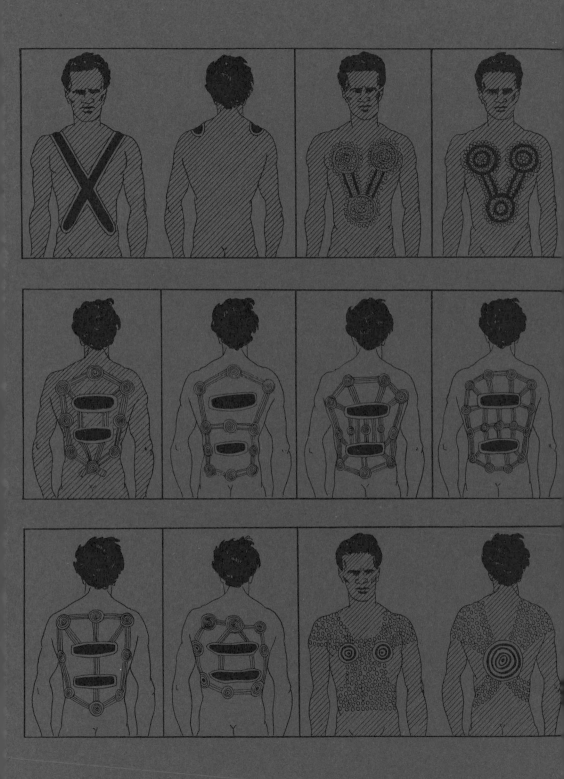